Street Lights
on the Path to Immortality

Brahmachari Sukshmamrita Chaitanya

Street Lights on the Path to Immortality
Brahmachari Sukshmamrita Chaitanya

Published By:
Mata Amritanandamayi Center
P.O. Box 613, San Ramon, CA 94583-0613 USA

In India:
www.amritapuri.org
inform@amritapuri.org

In Europe:
www.amma-europe.org

In US:
www.amma.org

VIMAL
മക്കളേ..

Contents

VIMAL

Contents

Aum Amriteshwaryai Namah

Preface

Since ancient times, Indian spiritual masters have taught their disciples profound spiritual principles using simple, relatable examples from their contemporary era. Likewise, Amma, the universal Guru of our time has also provided us with countless examples. After writing the Mahabharata, Sage Vyasa said, "What is in this book may be found somewhere in this world. However, what is not in this book cannot be found anywhere in the world." Let us try to correlate this with Amma. Nowhere else will we find clear, simple, and profound explanation of spiritual truths as those given by Amma. Be it Vedic texts or the history of the world, I do not think there is another Mahatma other than Amma who has given so many varied examples on every spiritual principle. This book you are holding is an example that illustrates this point.

Let me first note down what Amma said when I presented this compilation of Her jewels of wisdom to Her. Amma said. "Son, what you have done is very good. My children will develop more Shraddha (awareness) through reading these kinds of compilations. Amma is not saying that these teachings are good because Amma had said these. Amma's children can apply these in their daily lives. It is said that all we need to do is to listen carefully to the Guru's words. Paying attention to the Guru's words is required. However, with Amma, the relationship is more of a mother and children than a Guru and a disciple. Because the Guru's patience is the disciple's liberation.

Amma continued, "In this Kali Yuga, acting as a Guru is not going to get any disciples. The Guru must go to the level of the disciple to uplift them. The teachings given by Amma on different occasions are forgotten by my children. Many hear it through one ear and let it out of the other ear. Hence it is good to remember and record them down, to bring practical awareness in my children. This will benefit everyone. Therefore, the relevant context of the situation during which that example was narrated should also be recorded. Amma has narrated more than a thousand stories. It would be very good if my children's attention can be directed to spiritual principles through these stories. What Amma has said in the past has not been mentioned very often by my children in their satsangs or talks. Now they are paying attention and have started recording them. The need to do this has started growing in them now. This will be good for their spiritual growth, introspection, and help them guide others on the path.

We all have a 'matchbox' and 'matchsticks' inside of us. However, if the 'matchsticks' are damp, they cannot be of any use. It's only if they are dry can they be used to light lamps. We have within us the matchsticks of infinite capabilities and a matchbox. Unfortunately, these 'matchsticks' are wet – but the heat of awareness can make them dry. Similarly, a pen contains ink. However, if it is not used regularly, the ink will dry up and it cannot be used for writing. All these infinite powers exist within my children. That awareness has to be awakened and brought out internally and externally."

This book features stories and teachings from Amma's books and from what Amma has told me. Right from the beginning my seva at the ashram has been related to vehicles. Hence, I was attracted to Amma's examples relating to vehicles. When I started paying attention to these kinds of examples, it helped bring a radical change in my attitude towards life in general.

Amma does not have special liking or attachment to any vehicle. This book contains more than 63 of Amma's stories relating to vehicles extracted from my collection over the years; 63 'Roadside Lamps' to illuminate our journey through life. May this book serve as an inspiration to the readers to discover for themselves, many such pearls of wisdom from Amma relating to their own areas of work and life, and to compile and present them for the benefit of the world.

In the service of the Divine Mother,

Brahmachari Sukshmamrita Chaitanya

1. LIFE'S SITUATIONS AND OUR ATTITUDE

"Just as we adjust gears while driving a vehicle to navigate through road conditions like ups and downs, bends, turns, and traffic congestion, we must learn to adapt our attitude to face the challenging situations of life."

- Amma

Through this example, Amma teaches us that we should be ready to change our attitude when needed, to adapt to different situations in life.

When we travel, we see the driver changing gears from time to time. Depending on the road conditions, the driver must change gears to move forward quickly and safely. For example, he must change gears to drive slowly in areas with potholes, bends, turns, uphill areas, downhill areas, crowded markets, and busy roads.

(This does not apply to vehicles with automatic gears). Only if the gear is changed in such places, will the vehicle move forward smoothly.

Similarly, in life we cannot treat everyone the same way in every situation. People's attitudes and behaviors can vary based on positive or negative circumstances. Like changing gears in a vehicle, based on the situation, we need to adapt our attitude in a manner that benefits both us and others. It's important to understand the situation and respond with an attitude that is favorable for everyone involved.

That is why Amma says that our mental attitude has a great role to play in making our life joyous or sad. We enjoy experiences that please the mind. Whereas we face other experiences with disgust, sadness and sometimes anger. When you wear colored glasses, whatever you look at will take on that color. Likewise, we look at experiences through the lens of our likes and dislikes and interpret them as good or bad.

Amma says, “Suppose we have an old friend who has studied and worked with us for a long time. We may have supported this friend during their financial difficulties in the past. Now, when we face a financial crisis, we approach this friend with the hope of receiving assistance. However, things may not go as expected. This friend may not recognize us, or he may pretend not to know us. Sometimes he may completely ignore us. When we ask for a loan of Rs.10,000, he might give us Rs. 20,000, exactly Rs.10,000, or just Rs. 5,000. Perhaps, he will not give us anything at all. He might even say, “In fact, I was hoping to borrow some money from you.” It is possible to move forward in life and maintain friendships only if you are aware of these possibilities. We should be prepared for any of these outcomes. Otherwise, we will only experience sorrow and disappointment.

Our preferences greatly influence our perception. When we truly like something or someone, we tend to praise them wholeheartedly. For example, if a man is fond of a girl who may not be conventionally beautiful, he will see her as exceptionally beautiful. On the other hand, if there is someone he dislikes, regardless of their beauty, he will only notice their flaws. Our preferences unconsciously shape our thoughts, words and actions.

I remember a story Amma once told, "A woman heard a song on the radio while working in the kitchen and said to her husband, 'This song is so good, I feel like stopping all my work and listening to this song.' The husband asked, 'Do you know who is singing this? It is our neighbor who complained about you.' Hearing this, the wife's face changed, and she started criticizing the song saying, 'Hey! This song is not all that great. The singer is going off-key and going off the rhythm.'"

So, it is our mind that makes any experience good or bad. This tendency often hinders our ability to accurately evaluate various experiences in life. Our likes and dislikes can even affect the decisions we make in important situations. Therefore, it becomes essential to train our mind to respond wisely, to go beyond our passing preferences and whims, in order to make sensible choices.

Amma provides a couple of examples to illustrate this point, "When traveling in a bus, passengers often accidentally bump into each other. However, no one gets angry. We take it in stride because we know that it is unintentional and unavoidable in a crowded bus. So, we don't lose our temper towards these people.

By keeping our goal in mind and properly understanding the situation, we can control our anger. We all have the ability to think and control our minds. If we fail to use this ability effectively, we might assume that the passenger intentionally bumped into us, leading to anger and a desire for revenge. This can escalate into a fight.

"If a psychopath hits us, would we respond by hitting him back? No, we would show mercy and maturity because we understand his mental state to some extent. Having the right level of maturity enables us to respond by considering the other person's state of mind.

"Sometimes our minds seem calm. But when a situation arises, the dormant anger and revenge will surface, and we act without awareness. We react violently without even thinking for a moment. A snake lying frozen in the snow of the Himalayas may seem harmless to us. But if we pick it up, within no time it may try to attack.

"Our mind is like this. In adverse situations our mind will lose its capacity for discernment. What really matters is our maturity and discretion.

"This maturity is to be attained through meditation, prayer and spiritual pursuits. For that, spiritual thought and sadhana (spiritual practices) must be as much a part of life as eating, sleeping, and breathing. Fasting and religious rituals performed once-a-year during festivals and special days do not necessarily give us the strength to survive situations. Thus, spirituality is not just something to be practiced occasionally. Children, always remember that spirituality should always be with us, in our hearts, like a best friend. This is the purpose of all pujas, prayers and pilgrimages."

2. THE GREATNESS OF SATSANG

"Just like a single rain shower can wash away the dust from the leaves of roadside trees, listening to a satsang can purify our mind - no matter how impure it may be - and help us attain sattvic bhava."

- Amma

Amma shows us the greatness of satsang (spiritual discussion) through the following example.

While traveling on rural roads, if we observe the trees and billboards by the roadside, we will notice that they are all covered with dust. But no matter how many days of dust have accumulated, a single good rainfall will wash it all away. Similarly, when we interact with people, conflicts and arguments may arise, leading to anger and hatred that disturb our inner peace. Negative emotions like anger and hatred may affect the mind's tranquility. In such moments, if we have the opportunity to listen to a good satsang, all the impurities within us will be washed away, restoring calmness to the mind.

Let's hear more about Amma's perspective on this matter.

"In the present age, people tend to harbor hate towards others and themselves. Even small things can easily disturb someone emotionally. The constant desire to be the first and excel is a common mindset among both ordinary individuals and the privileged. Unfortunately, even minor setbacks in life can push people to the point of contemplating suicide. This is where the spiritual principle of self-love becomes crucial. Loving oneself doesn't mean being obsessed with our ego; it means appreciating and cherishing this human life as a precious gift. Additionally, it's important to acknowledge our own strengths and weaknesses. In order to overcome our weaknesses, we need to be aware of them and strive to transcend them.

"Haven't you heard of athletes who break their own records when no one else can surpass them? Each victory pushes these stars beyond their own limits. The Mahabharata tells the story of Arjuna practicing archery in the dark. Arjuna was inspired to do this by seeing his brother Bhima eating food in the dark. It sparked this idea in Arjuna's mind: 'Due to constant practice, our hand puts food in our mouth accurately even in the dark. Then why not practice archery in the dark, aiming at a target?' Here Arjuna competed with himself and triumphed, surpassing his mental limitations.

"If we wish to take on similar challenges and overcome our own limitations, we must keep our mind and intellect pure. We must cultivate positive thoughts and perform good deeds.

"In today's society there is a common belief that life revolves only around enhancing our physical appearance and indulging in sensual pleasures. We dedicate significant time every day to beautify and maintain the body. Visiting a beauty parlor, for example, requires us to sit patiently for hours. How much money, time, and effort we spend on it.

“Both children and adults spend considerable time in front of the mirror when they get up in the morning. Amma does not say that these activities are unnecessary. However, if we spare some time to cultivate the beauty and well-being of our minds, it will make our whole life beautiful.

“We follow a disciplined diet and exercise routine to prevent illnesses and achieve weight loss. However, even if our body is healthy and attractive, a weak and unhealthy mind can undermine its well-being. Therefore, it is crucial for us to recognize the importance of taking care of our mental health along with our physical health.

“In today's world, it has become a common practice for people to invite and dwell on unwanted thoughts, inadvertently nurturing them.

“A person wearing glasses was reading the newspaper in the morning. He first held the newspaper close for a while and tried to read it. Then he looked at it from a distance. After that, he tried reading it from different angles. His neighbor, observing him struggling so much to read the newspaper asked, ‘What happened, aren't the glasses right? Maybe it's time to change the lens - that’s why you are struggling so much.’ The first man replied, ‘Actually

I don't need reading glasses.' The neighbor retorted, 'Then, why are you wearing glasses?' The man replied, 'It was a pair of glasses that I found lying on the sidewalk during my morning walk. I just put them on to see if they would be useful in future.'

"Many people nowadays are like this man who wears glasses that he doesn't need and then struggles unnecessarily. If someone without any specific eye issues tries to read with glasses, it can actually have a negative impact on their vision. Similarly, indulging in unwanted thoughts can harm the well-being of the mind, leading to a loss of peace and tranquility."

"Self-discipline and inner purity are essential to overcome one's weaknesses; live life to the fullest and turn it into a blessing. Just as you take care of your body, take good care of your mind. Cultivate good thoughts. In that way, you can enrich your own life and the lives of others around you."

Why has Amma given so much importance to satsang? To give an example, let us imagine we come to see Amma when our mind is disturbed. When we reach the ashram, Amma's satsang is going on. Amma says, "Children, you must develop an attitude of accepting everything." When we contemplate on this, we realize that by accepting only what we like, we will not get all that we really need. If we go after only our likes, it will hinder our spiritual growth.

We are told to choose this attitude so that we do not lose our peace of mind. For example, suppose a crow pooped on us while we were walking. Will we hate that bird? No. Why is that? When we realize that the bird has no discretion, and it is pointless to hate it, we will achieve the mental state of acceptance.

Having such an attitude allows us to learn valuable lessons even from our adversaries. Our enemies are the ones who often highlight our weaknesses. If there is an attitude of acceptance, we can view it as a lesson. Trying to learn only from those who love us may not help us reach perfection. By considering the words of our enemies as a test, we can transform our attitude and enhance our mental strength.

When listening to good satsang, the animosity we had held within, as well as any ill feelings towards others, vanish. Just as the rainfall washes away the dust from the leaves, our minds are also cleansed of impurities. That's what Amma says, "If you listen to a good satsang, all the negativities we carry within us will be transformed." Here, satsang doesn't solely mean a speech or a lecture, but also includes the presence of a Great Mahatma.

3. IMPORTANCE OF SADHANA IN SOLITUDE.

"When learning how to drive, you should first learn in an open field. Once you have mastered the skill, you can safely drive on busy roads. Similarly, in the initial stages of meditation practice, we must find a secluded place. Once we have mastered meditation, then other noises will not disturb us."

- Amma

When we start learning to drive, we may struggle to control the vehicle properly. It will be dangerous for us and others if we choose to learn driving on the open road, as we might hit other vehicles or people. It is better to start in a deserted place until we understand and learn how to drive. There will be no problem for us and others when we embark on the road later. Once we have mastered driving, we can safely drive on any road.

We should apply the same principle in the beginning stages of meditation. One who tries to meditate should choose a secluded place. Otherwise, the surrounding noises will disturb our mind. The mind is distracted by what it sees and hears. Proper meditation does not take place there. For example, if we try to meditate in a busy marketplace where trade is happening, we may hear someone saying that the price of tomatoes has dropped. Then leaving the subject of meditation, our mind will wander, thinking, 'I wonder what caused the price of tomatoes to decrease?' The thought process may go on as follows: 'They may not be locally sourced tomatoes. Maybe the tomatoes are of bad quality. That's why the prices are so low...' Suddenly we see our thoughts and ask, 'Why am I thinking this? I have no need to buy tomatoes. Am I not sitting to meditate?' This realization prompts us to refocus on meditation, and we try again to ignore such distractions. This is what our meditation is like. To prevent such distractions, it's preferable to move away from such places and practice meditation in solitude.

Let's see Amma's observations relating to this. "Many people have different views about meditation. A few of the common misconceptions about meditation are as follows. Some believe that meditation involves closing your eyes and engaging in intense breathing exercises, or holding your breath unnecessarily. Some expect to see colors and lights or have heavenly experiences during meditation. However, these experiences, while they may occur, do not define meditation itself. True meditation is the state of calmness in the mind, an attitude of equanimity towards both pleasure and pain. It's a continuous experience.

"The monkey that is the human mind is more mischievous than real monkeys. The monkey in the forest jumps from the top of one tree to another. The human mind takes even greater leaps; it leaps higher than any other being. One minute it is here, the next minute it goes to America. From there it could go to the Moon, to the bottom of the sea, or become a millionaire. It travels between the past and the future in a split second. The goal of meditation is to subdue this restless mind and attain perfect calmness.

“If we have the TV’s remote control, we can switch to any desired channel or turn it on or off as needed. Like that, the remote control of the mind should be in our hands. That's what meditation is for. It is the way to maintain a continuous harmony between a still mind and actions.

“One can experience the true benefits of meditation only through continuous and sincere practice. Meditation should be practiced by sitting in a posture of your choice with a straight back and folded legs in your preferred asana (pose). Place your hands straight on your knees. If your legs become uncomfortable, you can get up and walk around or lie in Shavasana. Then, you can resume meditation. When lying down in Shavasana, it's important to stay awake and maintain an alert mind. Meditation can be practiced in any suitable asana or even while sitting on a chair, for those who are unable to sit with folded legs on the floor. Those who cannot do this, can practice meditation even while lying down. But be careful not to fall asleep.

"Make a habit of meditating daily, even for a short time. Through meditation, both the mind and the body have to be trained to be still. In the beginning, it may not be possible to sit for a long time. Gradually, keep increasing the meditation time by five or ten minutes. With constant and consistent practice, it is possible to forget everything and sit and meditate for hours at a time. As we delve deeper into meditation, it becomes our natural state. In the highest state, all actions become meditative. Unwanted thoughts will cease, and the mind will stop running after unnecessary desires. The realization will arise that true peace and happiness are inside of us.

"Once there was a bird on a ship sailing the deep sea. After spending several days at sea, the bird grew eager to reach the shore. Desiring to reach land, it flew east. But even after flying a great distance, it could not see land. Realizing the futility of continuing in that direction, the bird changed course and flew south. Not seeing land, it turned westward. Exhausted after flying in all directions like this, the bird returned to the ship and sat on the mast, enjoying some rest. Sitting and waiting there patiently, it eventually reached the shore without having to make any effort. The mind is like the bird in this story. It is constantly chasing after every wish and unfulfilled dream. When desire transforms into greed, control of the mind is lost, resulting in loss of happiness and peace. It is contemplative action and the attitude of compassion that enrich our lives. We should not forget this truth while pursuing material pleasures.

"Once your meditation practice is set and the mind is within your control, then you can meditate in any busy marketplace. It is like driving on a busy road after learning to drive."

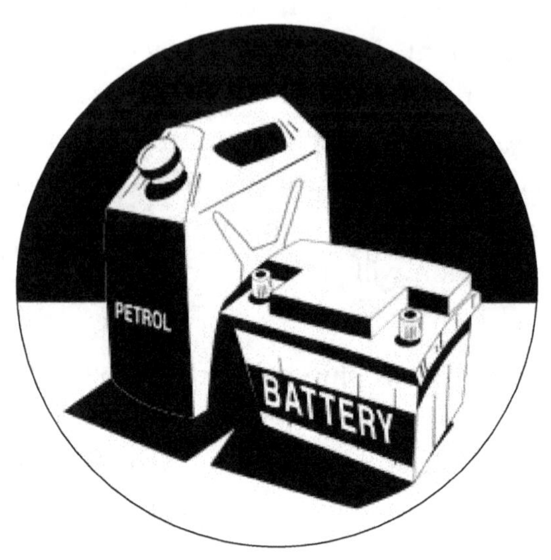

4. SELF-CONFIDENCE - THE INNER BATTERY

"A car needs a battery to start, even if it has petrol.
Similarly, success in life requires self-confidence
in addition to all other qualities."

- Amma

A vehicle, regardless of its fuel type, be it petrol, diesel, or gas, moves forward only after it has been started by the battery. Self-confidence plays a similar role in our lives. It is possible to encounter challenging situations in any sphere of life. In such instances, confidence is essential to help us move forward. Some circumstances can become unbearable and paralyze the mind. Self-blaming thoughts like, 'I cannot move one more step' or 'I am weak', can drain our morale. This is where self-confidence becomes necessary. What we need is the knowledge that the Almighty, Omnipresent, Omniscient God, or Guru, is with us. That self-confidence empowers us to surmount obstacles and forge ahead.

Amma often tells a story to highlight this: "Once, there was a man struggling to pull his cart out of a deep ditch with the help of one of his blind horses. Despite the horse's best efforts, the cart remained stuck, unmoving. At that moment, the cart man exclaimed loudly, 'Hey, Benny, lend a helping hand.' Upon hearing this, the blind horse gained a surge of confidence, thinking that his companion horse named Benny was now hitched to the cart. The horse thought to himself, 'I couldn't do it alone, but now that Benny is here with me, we can pull this cart out quickly.' Thinking this, the horse applied extra strength and pulled the cart out of the pit."

Similarly, we are never alone in our journey through life. When we realize that God, or Amma, is with us, our inner strength increases. When we face difficulties, we are able to overcome them and move forward.

That's why Amma says that "a mature mind is true spirituality. We may need property, savings, vehicles, and other material comforts in our life. But the purpose of human birth extends beyond the mere acquisition of these external achievements. True success in life is attained by developing the maturity to see ourselves in others. In one sense, achievements that are not based on this awareness can be considered failures, both for the individual and society.

"Success cannot be achieved through the development of skills alone. It is imperative to cultivate the ability to maintain a calm mind in any given situation. Without inner composure, even the most refined skills remain underutilized and fail to reach their full potential.

“Once a highly educated young man went for a job interview. The interviewer began by asking, ‘What is your name?’

“Gripped by tension, the young man remained silent for a while. Then he started chewing on his finger and humming a song.

‘Why aren’t you answering the question?’ asked the interviewer.

‘I was singing 'Happy Birthday to You.’ It has my name at the end.’

“Like this, stress can sometimes cause us to forget even our own name. No matter how talented we may be, our abilities cannot be effectively utilized unless our minds are calm and composed. A winner in the eyes of the world may, in reality, be a loser. On the contrary, a loser in the eyes of the world may, actually, be a winner. I have heard of an author, who gathered money and fame with his book on the subject of ‘how to achieve success in life.’ He ended his own life by committing suicide. Writing, reading, or preaching about success in life is not enough. These are of no use unless we bring our mind under our control.

“Once, there was a skilled archer who had won many competitions and eventually became the world champion. When a friend heard this, he challenged him by saying, ‘I know a spiritual master who is an expert in archery. If you can defeat him, I will recognize you as the true world champion.’ Intrigued by the proposition, the archer agreed to accompany his friend to the Guru's ashram. When he saw them, the Guru stood up and received them. The friend said, ‘Master, he is the world champion in archery,” and the Master congratulated the archer. Then the friend informed the Master of the purpose of their visit. On hearing this, the Master said, 'Let's go for a walk.' The Guru reminded the archer to bring along his bow and arrow.

"They walked for a while until they reached the summit of a tall mountain. There was a suspension bridge made of ropes connecting the mountain they were on to another. A wide river was flowing beneath. All three of them walked onto the suspension bridge. When they reached the middle of the bridge, the Guru said, 'That tree on the opposite bank has only one fruit. Can you shoot the fruit down with an arrow?' As the World Champion took aim at the fruit, the rope bridge started swaying violently in the wind. He worried about the possibility of falling into the river below. His entire body started trembling with fear. He managed to control his fear and shoot, but the arrow missed the target. When it was the Guru's turn, he took up the bow and took aim with astonishing calmness. The bridge was still swaying dangerously. But he aimed the arrow and hit the target, making the fruit fall. The 'remote control' of his mind was in his hand. Nothing external could disturb his mind, which is why he did not feel any fear.

"Can a dancer maintain peace of mind while performing on a constantly shaking stage? Facing life with a restless mind is similar to this. Only one thing remains constant —God. When we establish God as the foundation of our lives, our minds become still. This stillness itself is God. We should perform life's dance on the worldly stage firmly fixed on the stillness that is God. We will be able to accept life without fear or doubt, when we have the unwavering belief that God is always there to provide support and refuge. It will make our journey through life enjoyable. We can also spread happiness to others.

"In times of crises, we are the ones who let go of God. Not the other way around. God can never give up on us."

There was once a devotee who lived a life of complete faith and devotion to God. Leading his life in constant remembrance of God, he had the fortune of knowing God's presence near him. As life went on, a period of immense hardships completely shattered him. Though continuing to fervently pray to God, he started doubting if God was with him during this difficult time. Going to sleep with this thought, he saw a clear visual representation of his life's journey thus far, in a dream. In that dream, God's footprints were always visible next to his own. However, upon reaching the recently passed critical time in his life, he noticed only one set of footprints, which demoralized him further. The devotee started crying out loudly, "God, have you abandoned me at this moment of huge crisis in my life? Have you forsaken me?" He continued to lament, "How could you leave me at this critical juncture after walking with me for so long?" At this point, he heard a gentle and comforting voice, "My child, I have never left you. I have always been by your side. Those two footprints you saw were not yours, but mine. Look closely how they are deeply imprinted in the earth. I was carrying you in my arms when you were on the verge of falling."

Likewise, we must have unwavering confidence that God is with us during times of immense crisis.

5. FALSE PRIDE

"When we drive with headlights on, the light reflecting on signposts helps us see the road. Similarly, all our actions are empowered by God. Taking pride in our power is like the signboard saying proudly, "You are driving by my light."

- Amma

All actions in the world are solely driven by the power of God, yet we often assume a feeling of "doer-ship" for every action, leading to feelings of anxiety, worry, and tension.

When we travel at night, the light from our vehicle illuminates the signboards along the road, helping us understand the route and distance to our destination; we use this information to reach our goal. These signboards are often designed with reflective paint so that drivers moving at high speeds can easily read them.

So, the signboards reflect light. Where did the light that is reflected by these sign boards come from? It originates from the vehicle. Without understanding this, if the signboard claims, "You travel by seeing my light," isn't it merely a display of pride on the part of the signboard?

Amma makes this point clear to us through many examples. Amma says we are like this signboard. Whatever actions we do in life, it is accomplished through the power of God. However, without recognizing this truth, we often claim proudly, 'It is my ability that made all this happen.' Amma says, "Pride is a major obstacle to attaining God-realization, and it is our own creation. When such a person obeys a realized master, he has to put aside his likes and dislikes, and thus his pride diminishes gradually. Destruction of pride is in fact liberation."

Once upon a time a poet wrote a beautiful poem. It received immense recognition and numerous awards. On learning this, the ink in the poet's pen said, "I wrote that poem." The pen said, "No, it was I who wrote that poem." Then, the paper said, "Where would you have written that poem if I wasn't there?" In truth, the pen, paper, and ink are merely instruments in the hands of the poet. Similarly, the poet is just an instrument in the hands of God, as are all of us.

Amma often receives complaints from her children that even with sincere hard work and prayers they do not receive God's grace. However, Amma says, 'God's grace is always flowing towards us. It is we, who obstruct the reception of that grace with our pride and selfishness. Our state is like the satellite that cannot escape the gravitational pull of the Earth. The satellite needs booster rockets to transcend the Earth's gravitational field. Grace, knowledge, and devotion are the booster rockets that help us overcome our ego.

"Even the actions we consider trivial can be done only with God's grace. To close our mouth after yawning, it requires the proper functioning of the muscles controlling that action. Without this we would be unable to close our mouths. From this we can understand how our body, mind, and intellect are not entirely under our control. A man descending from the first floor of his house called out to his friend, 'Wait, I am coming down.' But by the time he had gone down a few steps, he collapsed and died of a heart attack. This shows us how even our next breath is not our hands. It is the power of God that guides us. Understanding this truth, we should have the attitude, 'I am only an instrument in the hands of God. It is God's power that enables me to act.'

"Vishwamitra was a great ascetic. His only wish was to become better than the revered Sage Vasishta. Sage Vasishta was more respected than Vishwamitra. Even after much contemplation, Vishwamitra could not understand why this was so. His mind became clouded with anger, resentment, and jealousy. To find an answer to this Vishwamitra approached Brahma one day and inquired, 'I have done penance for such a long time. I created a secondary heaven for Trishanku by the power of my penance alone. Yet, everyone respects Vasishta more than me. What is the reason behind this?' In response, Brahma advised 'Take Vasishta along with you and go see Anantha. He will clear your doubts.'

"According to ancient belief, the earth is supported by the cosmic serpent, Anantha. Vishwamitra explained everything to Anantha. Anantha listened to him and said, 'I am tired of bearing the weight of the earth. Please hold it for a while.' Vishwamitra said 'Holding the earth is as effortless as lifting a blade of grass for me.'

Saying so, Vishwamitra ventured to take the earth in his arms.

"Even as Anantha tried to place the earth in Vishwamitra's hands, Vishwamitra fell down unconscious, unable to bear the weight. After some time, Vishwamitra regained consciousness. Then Anantha asked Vasishta to hold the earth for a while. 'May the power that sustains me, that guides me, that acts through me, may that same power support this earth,' prayed Vasishta, extending both his hands very humbly. He was able to hold the earth's weight without any difficulty. Vishwamitra was astonished by this sight. Anantha then explained, 'Vishwamitra, your penance is unparalleled. But you have the attitude, 'I am doing this'. Whereas Vasishta performs actions with the awareness that 'God is doer. God acts through me.' That is the greatness of Vasishta. And the reason why everyone respects him.'

"All the sorrows we experience in life are due to our pride and selfishness. Only when the sense of 'I' and 'mine' is eliminated can we experience real happiness and peace. Only if the outer shell of the seed is broken, will it sprout and grow into a full-fledged tree that will provide shade for everyone in the future. Similarly, the shell of our pride must be broken. Only then can we become recipients of God's grace and grow fully."

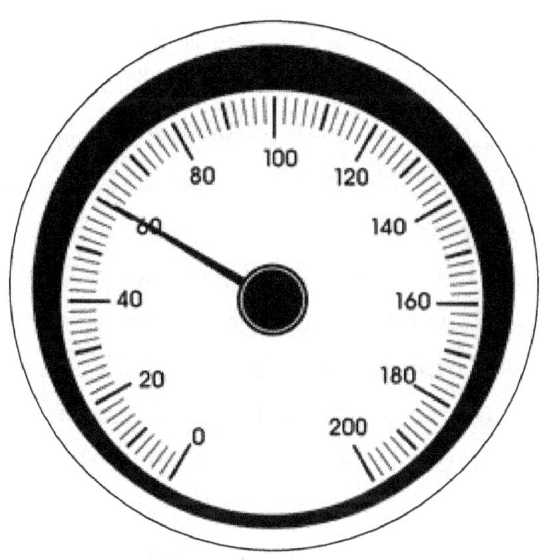

6. MODERATION

"Manufacturing companies set a speed limit on new busses, capping it at 60 kmph. Driving too fast in the initial stages can damage the engine of the vehicle. The speed has to be increased gradually over time. Similarly, in the initial stages of spirituality, if meditation and chanting are done excessively, adverse effects can cause the head to become hot."

- Amma

Through this example, Amma is advising that a sadhak should not meditate excessively during the initial stage of sadhana. Such unrestrained meditation can sometimes lead to mental discomfort.

At least some of those on the spiritual path will spend a lot of time in meditation at the beginning, due to their enthusiasm.

After a few days, you see them expressing discomfort due to their head getting heated. Sometimes loss of sleep happens in the initial stages. Although the desire for spiritual progress exists, time should be given for the body to align itself. It is to develop inner purity that the ancient texts prescribe Karma Yoga along with other practices. When an ordinary person turns to the spiritual path, it is essential to first strive for inner purity. No one in the world can refrain from performing actions. When we act with awareness, and without attachment to outcomes in our lives, the karmic imprint from past lives gradually gets reduced, and the mind becomes more and more pure. By doing this consistently, one's mind and body become suitable for higher levels of spiritual practices. This is a tradition that has been followed in India since ancient times.

Back then, those who went to study in Gurukulas had to perform many tasks like collecting firewood, fetching water, cleaning the ashram and its surroundings, and caring for the cows. Only after much time was spent like this would training in scriptures and meditation start. Calculating his mental and physical abilities during this time, the Guru would then give instructions on the duration of meditation and japa, and the appropriate breathing pattern to use. Meditation was started in the initial stages based on these specific instructions.

Amma says, "The purpose of human birth is to realize God. The ancient sages and scriptures have suggested various methods to reach this goal. Sanatana Dharma does not prescribe one path for everyone. Not everyone likes the same clothes or the same food. One-size shoes do not fit everyone. Similarly, one kind of spiritual practice will not suit everyone. Moreover, it may cause various physical and mental problems in some practitioners. Therefore, the practice of spiritual sadhana should be under the guidance and supervision of a self-realized master.

Gurus are those who have realized the Truth. Their words have the weight of experience. They know from experience what mode of sadhana is appropriate for whom. Just by looking at a person, a Guru can discern whether meditation, japa, prayer or pranayama would be best for them. The Guru advises a suitable spiritual discipline, taking into account each one's mental level, innate aptitude and physical capability."

Here is what Amma generally says about sadhana in the present time,

"The real learning is concentration of the mind. One can meditate focusing either on the heart center or the point between the eyebrows. But it is best to meditate on the heart center until one can sit comfortably and peacefully in one specific pose. One can practice meditating between the eyebrows when the Guru is present because the Guru knows what to do if, after meditation, the head gets heated up, or if you experience pain or pressure in the head, or in some cases, sleeplessness.

"Pranayama (practice of breath control) can be beneficial for some people. However, practicing it may pose risks for others. As such, those with heart disease and high blood pressure should be especially careful while doing pranayama. The Guru will give them the necessary advice based on these factors. Before prescribing pranayama to the disciples, the Guru will observe their natural breathing rhythm very closely. Only after that will he decide if pranayama should be advised. If it is advised, he will show the correct manner and intensity.

"The three components of Pranayama are Rechaka (exhalation), Kumbaka (breath retention) and Puraka (inhalation). Kumbaka is either exhaling completely and not letting out any more breath or inhaling deeply and holding the breath for a short while. This may not be suitable for some. Overdoing kumbaka will make the head hot. Tonic is good for health. But it is dangerous if we drink the entire contents of the bottle instead of taking the prescribed two spoonfuls. Similarly, practicing kumbaka beyond the recommended sequence will cause insomnia due the head becoming hot. Depression and other mental illnesses can happen. If fire is used carefully, food can be cooked. If it is handled carelessly, it can burn down the house and those in the house. Any object handled without proper understanding of its good and bad qualities can be dangerous to both to oneself and others.

"If you go the doctor, as part of screening, you will be asked to hold your breath and release it a certain number of times. There is an order to it. Similarly, pranayama also has a sequence. There are a few things to keep in mind while practicing pranayama and meditation. Instead of sitting on the bare floor, use a mat or spread a blanket and then sit on it. The spine should be straight. Do not wear tight clothes. Loosen the waist of the pants. Similarly, do not meditate or do pranayama immediately after eating food. The food will not be digested properly, and sometimes vomiting may occur. The duration of meditation and pranayama should be increased only gradually. However, regular practice of breathing exercises that do not involve kumbaka and simple meditation techniques help maintain physical and mental well-being, as well as spiritual growth.

"In general, spiritual practices such as prayer, archana, bhajans (devotional song), manasa puja (visualized worship) and japa (mantra repetition), can be done by anyone. However, moderation is required in any of these because the human body has limitations. Awakening the dormant infinite spiritual power within us must be done with utmost care. Otherwise, physical and mental difficulties may arise. Doesn't the bulb blow a fuse when too high of a current passes through it? Therefore, one should gradually awaken that power through spiritual practices in a way that the body, mind, and intellect can withstand. Try to practice these sadhanas daily at a specific time. Slowly increase the duration. Thus, over time, one can develop the ability to do spiritual practices at any time and for any length of time. Spiritual practices based on knowledge of these principles can give meaning to life, safeguard health and mental peace, and help us develop the right outlook on life."

7. SOME POINTERS

"During the road journey, when we see a sign that says, 'Road construction is in progress, use caution', we develop the patience to slow down. Likewise, if we understand that anger is a sign of someone's inner distress and agitation, we get the patience to exercise self-control in that situation."

- Amma

We all have the ability to forgive. We have to use it when the situation requires it.

In our travels, we have all had to pass through road construction areas. We get the patience to slow down as soon as we see signboards indicating this. Similarly, we should slow down when somebody is angry with us. The 'roadwork' of agitation and anxiety is going on inside him. The anger he expresses is the warning signal of his mental state. When understand this, we gain the strength to forgive him.

Let us see what Amma says. . .

"There is no one who has not made mistakes in life. It can be said that life is a journey from wrong to right. Everyone forgives his own mistakes. We may even forgive mistakes made by our own children. However, if others do us wrong, it is difficult for us to tolerate it. We may lose self-control and lash out at them immediately. If not, we retain the grudge and hatred grows inside us. We can find many people around us who harbor dislike and resentment towards neighbors, co-workers and even their siblings, over trivial matters. We don't realize that these emotions are more harmful to us than anyone else. If someone knowingly hates or harms us, they are showing their weakness. They are like sick people. We don't hate people who are suffering. If a madman insults us, we will forgive him by understanding his condition. If a crow defecates on us, do we get angry at the crow, or do we just clean it up?

"In fact, our sorrows are not the creation of others. They arise either as a result of our past actions, or as a result of our current wrong attitude. When others act against us, we should happily accept that as an opportunity to exercise our mental strength and mental harmony. But there are many of us whose situation is pathetic. We carry hatred for others for twenty or even thirty years, over trivial matters, continually cursing them, picking fights with them and finding faults.

"A man was bitten by a dog on his way home from work one evening. At first, he didn't give it much importance. He didn't go to see a doctor. Days passed and finally, he went to the hospital, where he became very sick and weak. The doctor said, "I suspect that you have been bitten by a rabid dog. Since so many days have passed, your condition has become very serious, and it is impossible to cure it." On hearing this, the man took a piece of paper and began to scribble something on it with much seriousness. Seeing this, the doctor felt very sad and compassionate. The doctor said, 'Are you writing a will? You don't need it right now. A few new medicines have come out. If you take them, it is possible to live for a few more days.' The doctor tried to console him very lovingly and compassionately. Then the patient said, 'Who said I am writing a will? I have only a few more days to live. Every second of my life is very precious. So, I am making a list of my enemies. I will bite as many of them as I can before I die to take revenge.'

"We should not be like this. God has given us only a short time on this earth. We should share it happily, by loving helping and comforting each other. We should understand that God will forgive our mistakes only if we are ready to forgive others' mistakes.

"We should be able to feel peace and tranquility even while living in society. It is of no use to experience peace only when sitting in solitude in a forest. Patience and endurance are required for this. Do we get angry with our teeth if we accidentally bite our tongue while eating? No. The teeth and tongue are parts of our own body. Similarly, we need to rise to a state where we can tolerate and forgive the faults and shortcomings in others, knowing that the same divine spirit that gives us life resides in them as well. Human life itself is for that purpose.

"Life is like a flower garden. It is natural for leaves to dry up and flowers to wither and fall off. It is only if we remove the decayed matter at the right time that will we be able to fully enjoy the beauty of the flower garden with its new flowers and new growth. So, let us wipe clean the mental impurities created by our past. Let us forgive what needs to be forgiven. Forget what needs to be forgotten. Embrace life with renewed awareness."

8. ABHYASENA TU KAUNTEYA! (BY PRACTICE, O ARJUNA!)

"Lack of discrimination in situations that require it, even after studying Vedanta, is like someone who has studied automobile engineering and yet, is unable to repair his own vehicle."

- Amma

Through this example, Amma is saying that merely knowing how to recite Vedanta is not enough. We must live by those principles.

If a person who has studied automobile engineering travels with us, and he does not know how to repair our vehicle when it breaks down on the road, then what purpose does his education serve? Likewise, if one cannot control the mind in critical situations, then what is the point of studying Vedanta?

Amma illustrates this with many examples.

"In today's society, we can see many who have studied Vedanta, who speak about Vedanta, who listen to talks about Vedanta... But how many of them have lived in the way mentioned in Vedic philosophy or have tried to apply it in life? The goal can be reached only if you live according to the Vedantic teachings. So, there is no difference between the words of such people and a tape recorder.

"The basic principle of spiritual life is Advaita (non-duality), to transcend above perceived differences. This is to be applied in every moment of life and not just talked about. Advaita limited to just words is perhaps the biggest downfall that could happen in spirituality. Unfortunately, today it is mostly such people that we find around us. This is like a tape recorder or like a trained parrot that repeats the words it was taught. Vedanta books are available in bookstores. There are those who go around saying, 'I am Brahman' after reading these. But there will be no decrease in negativities like anger and desire in them.

"Once a person came for darshan and said to Amma, 'Amma, I am a Vedantin (one who is immersed in Vedanta)'. Amma did not respond. That son said again, 'I am not this body, I am the atman, so no karma can affect me.' Amma remained silent. Then he loudly chanted, 'Aham Brahmasmi' two or three times. Still Amma did not say anything. After a being silent for a short while, he chanted, 'Shivoham' loudly a few times. Amma did not speak. As this went on, the person asked, 'Amma you have not said anything yet'. Then Amma said, 'Are you not Brahman? Then what is there for Amma to say?' That is when the person said, 'But, Amma, I am unable to control my anger, hatred and desires.' This is the type of Vedanta we see in today's world.

“Our scriptures speak of the third eye. Many are expecting it to appear between the two eyebrows. It is not going to happen like that. This third eye should open inside us. It is a state of seeing everything as one, where the distinction of “I” and “You” disappears even while both of our eyes are open. That is true Vedantic experience. This state of non-duality is what is mentioned as the third eye of Lord Shiva and Kali.

"Unpracticed Vedanta is like writing the word honey on a piece of paper and trying to taste the sweetness by licking it. Knowledge is good. But only when we apply it in life will it benefit us and society in general. Amma isn't criticizing or making fun of those learning Vedanta. Studying scriptures is indeed good. It is necessary. Advaita is the Supreme Truth. That is the foundation for everything, but we should apply it in our lives. Only if we understand and live by that principle can we move forward in any situation without getting disillusioned. When living in the world, practical Vedanta is doing all actions with equanimity and compassion. If our left hand hurts, our right hand will caress it because both are ‘mine’. Similarly, love others seeing their pain as our own; serve them.

“Only those who are firmly established in the Advaita principle will be able to perform selfless service. Service without expectations is seeing unity in diversity. When we look from the outside, selfless service may also seem to have the aspect of "I" and 'you'. But that is not reality. What a sculptor sees in a stone is the beautiful sculpture that can be carved out of it. Likewise, those who have integrated Vedanta into their lives serve the world seeing their own Self in everything. External changes, pleasures, sorrows, victories, or defeats do not affect them. They are like a gentle breeze that caresses everything uniformly. In fact, only such persons can uplift the world through selfless service.

"It is not Advaita, if after seeing the sorrow and misery of people who are suffering, someone refuses to offer comfort saying, 'I am the Atma. I am beyond all this.' Such individuals are neither Vedanta practitioners nor genuine religious believers. The study of Vedanta and religious belief is meaningless if it fails to comfort and dry the tears of those who are suffering, to selflessly become their solace and strength.

"A student of medical science (MBBS) is accepted as a doctor only upon completion of house-surgency or internship. Otherwise, it will remain as theoretical knowledge only. For one year they are required to work in hospital wards and engage with all kinds of patients. They must gather information from each patient and comprehend the medications and diets being prescribed by the other doctors. The mental and physical levels of each patient vary. Their treatments and diets will differ accordingly. This is how interns bring their theoretical knowledge to the practical level. Only then can they intelligently consult with patients and listen to description of illnesses with confidence. That's why Amma says that Vedanta studies must be brought to the practical level.

"No matter how much one learns about swimming from books, if one wishes to swim in a river one has to train in the water. As long as this is not done, it will remain as intellectual knowledge.

"Merely studying Vedanta texts does not automatically make someone a Vedantin. Vedanta should become life's philosophy. Vedic studies are good. But it is essential to contemplate deeply on those principles. With meditation they should penetrate the depths of the heart. They must be integrated into life. One should be able to transcend the limitations and weaknesses of the mind by this."

9. ANGER

"Arguing with the driver of the vehicle in front of us while stuck in traffic, is like getting angry when patience is needed."

- Amma

There are two types of situations that come to us in life. The first consists of those we can change. The second are those that cannot be changed. We must try to change the situations that can be changed and patiently accept those that we cannot change.

When we travel, our vehicle sometimes gets stuck in the middle of traffic. But some people do not understand this situation and can be seen fighting with the drivers ahead of him. There is no point in shouting at them. If the vehicle in front of us needs to move, either the traffic light must turn green or the vehicle in front of it should start moving. There are no other ways ahead except these two. Here there is no benefit in shouting. It just destroys the peace of the one shouting and the one getting shouted at.

This is what Amma says on this topic. “The one thing we need to pay special attention in life is controlling our anger. Anger is like a double-edged sword that wounds not only the target but also the one holding it. When we feel angry with someone, how disturbed our mind becomes! The mind is so restless that it is impossible to sit, stand or lie still. Blood heats up as anger increases. It will pave the way for non-existent diseases. If only we understood the inner changes that happen to us in the heat of anger.

“We may think many times before we even smile at someone. If I smile now, won't that become familiarity. Based on that familiarity, will he ask for some help tomorrow? Is he someone who needs money... Many people contemplate deeply over these things before even attempting to smile. But it is not so with anger. When we should be reflecting, we forget everything and get angry. Some justify their actions by saying, "It's just my nature to get angry. I can't control it." But this is not true. In some situations, we control ourselves. For example, no one usually gets angry with superiors at the workplace because they know that they will be punished. It may lead to a transfer or prevent a promotion. It could even mean a lost job. So, people maintain maximum restraint in such situations.

“At the same time, no one is seen to have any restraint in getting angry at their subordinates. This is where one really needs to control oneself because they can't say anything back to us. They are dependent on us. They may not visibly retaliate. But their hearts will be heavy, their mind may unwittingly say, ‘God, I have to listen to this scolding for a mistake I do not know anything about.

God, don't you see the truth...' The waves of grief rising from their hearts will becomes a curse against us. It is not easy to be liberated from that. Perhaps, they too may have hurt someone's heart before. Their pain can become a barrier to God's grace flowing to us.

"This does not mean that a supervisor should not reprimand in situations where it is needed. When you see mistakes, you need to correct them. Love and gentleness may not always work for everyone. When that happens, we can show seriousness. But the anger should be like a mask. Inwardly, we should not be troubled. And our anger should not be directed at the individual. It should be focused on the act of wrongdoing. We should not be angry unnecessarily or more than needed. Be especially careful not to hurt other people's hearts with your words.

"It is the nature of some people to take their anger out on someone else when they see that their opponent is strong. However, doing so will only make the problems worse.

"Once, long ago in a royal palace, the court jester was telling stories. Now and then he also cracked good jokes, but the king did not understand them. The king angrily hit the jester, mistakenly thinking that the jester was making fun of him. The clown writhed in pain. He gritted his teeth in anger. However, because the one who beat him was the king, he could not say another word. So immediately the clown slapped the person standing next to him. The person asked the jester, 'Why did you do that? I didn't do anything to you. Why did you hit me?' The jester replied, 'I have only shared with you the gift that the king gave me. You can slap the one who is standing next to you. Life is like a giant wheel. As it rolls, each one gets what he deserves.'

"If the clown had thought that what he experienced was his own karma, instead of thinking that what others were experiencing was the result of their karma, he could have forgiven the king's indiscretion. Instead, he added to his sins by harming others. We should always remember that anger is the seed of the tree of sin. If a madman abuses us, we forgive him. We forgive a child's mistakes as well. This is because we know that they are doing this out of ignorance. Mostly, the ego is the reason for our anger. We should be able to recognize this. Getting rid of anger is essential for success in life."

10. THE YAMA NIYAMAS: MORAL CODES AND THE SPIRITUAL SEEKER

"Vehicles need a road to drive on and traffic rules to follow. But birds don't need roads to fly nor any rules. Similarly, common people have to observe moral codes while living in society. But great souls may not act according to these rules. Ordinary people cannot imitate all of their actions."

- Amma

We know that for any vehicle to move, it needs roads that are appropriate for it and traffic rules to keep it safe. But birds do not need such rules or paths to fly. Mahatmas (self-realized masters) are like these birds. They may not always follow the Yamas and Niyamas (ethical rules) like ordinary people. They have already attained what is to be gained by following the Yamas and Niyamas.

Let's take Amma as an example. Amma's hallmark is to embrace and accept all those who approach her, regardless of gender, age, status, caste, religion, or nationality. Have we heard or read anywhere in the history of the world about another Mahatma who gives darshan like Amma and who personally listens to and solves the problems of so many people? Be it an administrator, a poor man, a rich man, an old man, a small child, a thief, a murderer, a prostitute, an Advaitan, a devotee, an atheist, a rationalist--anyone can come for Amma's darshan without any restrictions. What would be the situation if we tried to emulate this, after seeing that Amma has gained millions of followers and fame all over the world through her darshan alone?

Amma does not have to make a conscious effort to love anyone. Love manifests by itself; it happens organically. Amma cannot hate anyone. Amma knows only one language. It is the language of love. That is understood by all. The poverty the world is suffering from today is this lack of selfless love.

Let's see how Amma explains this: “Everyone talks about love. They say they love each other. But this cannot be called true love. Today, what we think of as love is adulterated with selfishness. It is like a gold-plated ornament. It looks nice when you wear it, but it does not have much value. And it will not last long.

"A sick child said to his father as they were leaving the hospital, "Dad! Everyone here likes me. The doctors, nurses, attendants, and watchmen are all so loving! They always inquire about me. They pay attention to all my needs. They make the bed and bring me food on time. They don't scold me. Do you love me as much as they do? How much you and mother scold me!” At that moment, the nurse brought a paper and handed it to the father.

Seeing this, the son asked what it was. Father said, "Didn't you just talk about their love? This is a bill for that love."

“This is the kind of love we see in the world today. Behind any love, one can see some selfish motive. The opportunistic attitude found in the market has permeated personal relationships. Whenever we meet someone, our first thought is what can we gain from them. If there is nothing to be gained, no relationship is established. When we stop getting what we want, relationships are broken. So much selfishness has filled human minds. Human society is experiencing the consequences of this today.

"Amma does not feel separate from whoever comes to her. She feels they are Amma's own self. Whenever there is a pain in our body, the hand will reach out to it as soon as possible to comfort it. Similarly, Amma has always feels the sorrow of others only as her own sorrow. Can a mother stand by and watch when a little baby cries in pain? Amma does not know how to love a person based on who they are. If a lamp is lit in the courtyard, everyone who comes there will get the same amount of light. There will be no differences in the amounts. But if we sit inside the room with closed doors, we will live darkness only. There is no point sitting there and finding fault with light. If you want light, you have to be ready to open the doors of your mind and come out.

"Amma only looks at the hearts of her children. Amma does not think about their wealth or material circumstances. No real mother can think of her children like that. But if a sad person comes to Amma, Amma will feel compassion. Amma will experience his grief as her own. Amma will do her best to give relief for his sorrow.”

Some people say only another Mahatma can understand a

Mahatma like Amma. The only way we can comprehend to some small extent is when we study the scriptures. Therefore, it is important to understand that although one can accept the teachings of great souls, one should not always imitate their actions.

11. WHEN IN ROME DO AS ROMANS DO

"In India, we drive on the left side of the road. But in the United States, it is on the right side. Similarly, the culture of the people is different from place to place. We should understand this and behave accordingly."

- Amma

Amma is making clear through this that we should always understand the nature of the society that we interact with and behave accordingly.

In India, vehicles are driven on the left side of the road because that is what is dictated by the road rules in India. So, obstinately saying that I will only drive on the left side of the road everywhere in the world will not work. If we are in the United States, we must drive only on the right side of the road as per the rules there.

When we go to a place, we should interact with the people there understanding their rules and their customs. Otherwise, it will bring us grief. We may even be insulted, or have to experience loss.

Let's see how Amma clarifies this further -

"Once a man, after reaching an unfamiliar place, thought that he would go to a tea shop and have tea. That tea seller was a man who stammered. As this man also had a stammering problem, he stammered while asking the shopkeeper for a tea. At first the tea seller did not say anything. When he asked for tea a second time with his stammer, the tea seller thought, 'he is making fun of me.' He slapped the visitor. The man who came to drink the tea did not understand the reason. So, he slapped him back. Like that while they were having a big fight, someone came and pulled them apart and asked what was the matter. Then the shopkeeper said, "He asked for tea twice, making fun of me. That's when I hit him." Then the person who came to buy the tea said, "I can only ask like that because I have a stammer.' The third person said to both, "You both have a stammer. That's what caused this fight." This will be the result if we act without understanding others.

Once someone asked Amma, "Amma, it is said that initially you had to face a lot of opposition. What does Amma have to say about it?"

"Amma replied, 'It doesn't seem like a serious matter to Amma. I knew the nature of the world. When we are at a temple festival, we know that fireworks can go off, so we don't need to get startled. A person who has learned to swim in the sea can enjoy swimming, even in the midst of the waves. He does not become afraid or weary when he sees huge waves. As Amma had already understood the nature of the world, the obstacles only served to delight me. All of those created the opportunities for me to look inwards. The naysayers became my mirror. I could only see them in that light. Sorrows and complaints occur only when we think that 'I am the body'. Sorrow has no place in the world of the Self.

"When I thought about the True-Self, I understood that I am not the pond, but the river. Many people come to bathe in the river. People who are sick and those who are not sick. Some drink its water. Some take a bath. Some do laundry. Some spit in it. No matter who uses its water and how, the river has no problem. It keeps flowing. It has no complaints whether used for puja or bathing. It keeps on flowing, caressing all. However, the pond water is not like that. Its water stagnates and gets decayed. Only an unpleasant smell can come from that. Once I thought of this, neither the oppositions I had to face nor the love I happened to experience, could create any emotion in me. It didn't seem to be all that important. Sadness arises when we identify with the body. But this sorrow has no place at the level of the Self. No one is separate from me. The shortcomings of others seemed to be my own. So, nothing felt like oppression. They threw mud at this tree, but it became a fertilizer for me. It was all for the best.

"Once when two friends met, one asked the other, 'What are you sad about? Is your business not going well?' The other said, 'It's going well here. However, the new branch we started in another country is a total loss.' His friend asked, 'What is the reason for that? Didn't you advertise well?' He replied, 'We advertised extensively, but without understanding the local culture of the people.'

'What went wrong?" his friend asked. 'We used the same advertisements that we had used here. There were three pictures in that ad. It's like this. In the first one, a person is sitting exhausted, with no energy. Then he gets this drink. In the third picture, he drinks it and is running with great energy. This was the advertisement.' 'Wow, that sounds like a great ad,' his friend said. 'Why didn't it work?' 'Well, my friend. The people there read from right to left. So, what they saw was - a person running at great speed. When he drinks the product, he sits down exhausted.' The loss came because they advertised without understanding the reading style of the people there."

12. FORESIGHT OF GURU

"When someone is teaching driving and a ball comes and falls on the road, what will he do? If he is skilled instructor, he will advise you to stop immediately because there might be children playing nearby. There is a chance that one of the children who was playing could come running after it. Similarly, a good Guru guides his disciples after foreseeing what is to come. The disciple may not have the ability to see these things in advance."

-Amma

If driving is taught by an experienced driving instructor, he can explain in advance the potential dangers that could occur in any situation. This is because the instructor has experience. They are doing this with the intent that "such a danger should not happen to my student." During a driving lesson, if a ball bounces onto the road, the instructor will ask the student to stop the vehicle immediately. Little children who are playing with the ball can come running onto the road. They will be focused only on the ball, not paying attention to anything else. So, if the vehicle does not stop ahead of time, they may jump in front of the vehicle. This can cause a serious accident.

Along these lines, a person asked Amma, "Amma is established in the Supreme-Self. If so, then why and to whom does Amma pray? What is the need for Amma to do any Sadhana?'

Amma replied like this,

"Amma has taken a body for the sake of the world, not for Amma's sake. Amma did not come to this world to claim, "I am an avatar" and not do anything. There is no point in taking birth if it were to sit idle! Amma's purpose is to guide people towards inner bliss. Amma came to demonstrate how people can be uplifted. If hearing or speech impaired people are in front of us, don't we also try to communicate matters to them using hand gestures or sign language? If we think 'I can hear properly. So why should I use sign-language?', hearing-impaired people would not be able to understand anything. Whatever you say, they need this sign language. Similarly, to uplift those who live without knowing who they are, we have to go down to their level. We have to live in front of them and show them. For them kirtan (singing divine names), meditation and seva (selfless service) are all necessary.

"Amma assumes many roles in order to uplift them. All these roles are for the benefit of the world. People come to the ashram by plane, train, car, bus, and boat. But Amma never asks, 'In what kind of vehicle have you come?' Each one finds their own way to get here according to their capabilities. Similarly, there are many ways to know the True-Self. Amma prescribes a method according to each one's samskara (innate tendencies). Those who are good at math are the ones who should take engineering in college because they can learn faster and advance quicker than others. Similarly, those who have the intelligence to read and understand scriptural texts may be able to reflect on 'neti, neti' philosophy, ('doctrine of neither this, nor that') at an intellectual level and move forward. Only those with scriptural education and subtle intelligence will be able to do that. This may not be possible for ordinary people. Those who come to the ashram for the first time may not even have heard of spirituality. What can children like this do? Shouldn't those who have no spiritual background also make progress? Shouldn't they also be uplifted? The upliftment has to be done after understanding the level each person is at and going down to that level.

"There are people who come for darshan here who do not know how to read. Poor people who can read but who have no money to buy books also come. There are those who have read and understood somewhat, and those who have read and comprehended much. There are some who understand, but are unable to apply the teachings in their lives. Each person must be guided according to the cultural background of their upbringing. 'Brahman' is not something to be expressed in words. It is an experience. It is life. It is a state of being that allows us to perceive others as an extension of ourselves. That has to become our normal state. When thinking of a flower, you have to become the flower. We all have to try to become a flower. We should be able to make Advaita our life. That's what learning should be for. It is not difficult to memorize something; the difficulty is to bring it into our actions.

"The concepts that the Mahatmas of the past have shown us

through their lives are studied, memorized, and debated by people today. Puja and prayers are faces of the same Brahmam. A Guru who has this kind of life experience teaches the disciple who is living with him through stories and examples.

"In an ashram, there was a woman who would come daily and water the plants and sweep the yard. Noticing this, the Guru immediately called his disciple and said, 'That woman coming here is not good for you. It will harm you, especially in my absence. It may affect your self-control. You must tell her not to come here from now on.' The disciple did not like this. The disciple said 'Master, isn't she an elderly and unattractive woman? What is the harm in her coming? I won't weaken like that.' The Guru remained silent. The following day, the Guru instructed his cook, 'Prepare a meal with excessive salt and deliver it to the disciple's room. Close off the water supply in the room. Also leave a bucket of water mixed with cow dung in his room.' The cook did all of these things. Subsequently, the Guru locked the disciple's room from the outside, took the key, and informed the disciple, 'You have to stay in this room. Do not walk outside. I am going away. I will return after two days.'

As the disciple finished the food and attempted to drink water, the tap did not work. At first, he sat without drinking water for a long time. Then he tried to leave the room in search of water, but the room was locked. After some time, his thirst became unbearable. When it became overwhelming, he drank the water mixed with cow dung that was in the room and quenched his thirst.

"On the second day, when the Guru came back and entered the disciple's room, he did not see the water mixed with cow dung. The Guru asked, 'Where is the water mixed with cow dung that was kept in this room?' The disciple replied, 'I drank it when my thirst became unbearable.' The Guru then remarked, 'Oh, do you drink cow dung water whenever you are thirsty? Do you like it that much?' The disciple replied, 'It's not because I love it, Guru. I was compelled to drink it when I could no longer endure my thirst.' The Guru said, 'See, you drank even such bad water when a situation arose. Such a thing can happen with women also, when we get caught in situations like this. That is why I told you that though the woman who comes to serve here is not beautiful, we should be careful not to create a similar situation.'

13. SEEKING TO COMPREHEND THE MAHATMAS

"Those traveling in a car with tinted windows can see the people outside. But the people outside will not be able to see the passengers. Likewise, it is not difficult for Mahatmas to understand others. But ordinary people like us cannot understand Mahatmas."

- Amma

Famous people often have cars with tinted windows to avoid drawing public attention. Certain types of glass are transparent from one side only. People outside a vehicle with such glass cannot see those inside, but the occupants can see those outside. Mahatmas are like this. They can know and understand others easily, but as ordinary people, we cannot understand them.

A Mahatma does not see anyone as different from himself. But we see a Mahatma as an individual separate from us. We cannot understand the mind of a Mahatma. But the Mahatma is able to know what is going on within us, just as they know their own thoughts.

This is what the Lord also says in Srimad Bhagavad Gita, Chapter 9, Verse 11:

> "avajānanti māṁ mūḍhā mānuṣhīṁ tanum āśhritam
> paraṁ bhāvam ajānanto mama bhūta-maheśhvaram"

Fools disregard Me when I dwell in human form; they know not My Higher being as the Great Lord of all beings.

In the Bhagavad Gita, when Arjuna asks Lord Krishna to describe the qualities of a Sthithaprajna (person of steady wisdom), he is asking how to recognize a Mahatma (a great soul). The qualities of such a soul are described in the Srimad Bhagavad Gita.

A 'Sthitaprajna' is one whose mind is unperturbed by sorrows, devoid of desires for material pleasures, and free from attachment, fear, and anger.

There are generally three types of sorrows in human life:

1) Adhyatmikam – related to oneself only, such as diseases arising from one's prarabdha (accumulated results of past actions) or environmental factors.
2) Adhibhautikam - suffering caused by the five elements or by other beings, thieves, riots, fire etc.
3) Adhidaivikam - challenges caused by natural disasters such as earthquake, Tsunamis etc.

The Mahatma is someone who is not troubled by any of these, who has no yearning for material things and is free from attachment, fear or anger towards anything.

They will act with steadfastness in the face of these three types of sorrows. We need not search for proof of this in scriptures or other books. Amma is the living example for us.

Once Amma was asked, "How can one who has not given birth be a mother?" Amma replied, "A Mother is a symbol of selflessness; a mother's life is to know her child's true heart and live for their sake. A mother will tolerate the child's mistakes. Because from a mother's perspective, a child does wrong only because of his ignorance. Mothers do not think that it is the child's arrogance. This is Motherhood. My life is also this. For Amma, all are children. Amma's only wish is that Amma's life should be like an incense stick. Even as the incense stick burns, it gives fragrance to others. Similarly, Amma only wants every moment of her life to be useful to her children. Amma does not see the goal and the means to attain it as two separate things. Life flows according to divine will. That's all."

Surely, Amma is the most publicly accessible Guru the world has ever seen. Perhaps Amma may be the only one who has maintained a personal connection with the greatest number of people in the world. Amma's life has been dedicated to personally listening to the problems of millions of people from diverse cultures worldwide, providing guidance and solace to them.

Many Mahatmas are reluctant to receive people burdened with negative tendencies. Even the mere touch of such people caused physical distress to Sri Ramakrishna. But Amma extends both her arms and embraces the people of the whole world. In fact, Amma's touch is nothing but a consecration through touch, bestowed by a perfect Guru.

Amma's darshan, where she embraces everyone regardless of their gender, has been the subject of criticism by some. Let's see what Amma herself says about this.

"Many today cannot embrace even their own birth mother with a pure attitude. Such is the state of their minds. However, a baby's mother feels only affection towards him. It is never lust. Likewise, Amma thinks of everyone as her child. If you ask why Amma hugs others, it can only be said that it is Amma's nature. For Amma, compassion is inherent. Just as sweetness became the nature of a ripe fruit, motherliness and compassion became Amma's nature. Amma does not feel any difference between men and women."

That is why it is very difficult for ordinary people to understand such Mahatmas.

14. WHAT IS THE OBSTACLE TO PROGRESS?

"On a narrow road, if each of the two vehicles coming from opposite directions think, 'You have to move, I won't move', neither will be able to go forward. It is our ego that obstructs our progress."

- Amma

Through this example, Amma is showing us that the only obstacle to our progress in life is our own ego.

Many of us have had the experience of having to pass through a narrow road or a narrow bridge during our journeys. Some large oncoming vehicles may not be able to pass. In such places, one of the vehicles will usually move to the side, or one of the drivers will reverse his vehicle to allow the oncoming vehicle to pass. Only after one vehicle has driven past can the other one move forward. But what happens if neither of them moves back? Both cannot go forward at the same time. Similarly, when there is a conflict between two people in any field, and if neither one is ready to compromise, their egos become a hindrance to their own progress. Here our own ego is making fools of us.

Amma says,

"Although everything is God's creation, the ego is our own creation. It is this ego that separates us from God. We know of many families that broke due to the ego of either the husband or the wife. Because of that, so many children are orphaned, they become addicted to drugs, alcohol, and violence. If one of the parents can be tolerant, their children can live so happily in their families. Similarly, our ego afflicts all areas of our life, and destroys the joy and beauty of life, in the same way that a worm gets into a garden and destroys the flowers and plants. That's why Amma says that ego is like a defective mold. To quickly produce many clay figures in the exact same shape, the sculptors first make a mold. However, what if there is a defect in that mold? All the products made with that mold will have that defect.

“Once a Major in the army got promoted to Colonel. When he reached this position, an immense sense of pride seized him. He realized that he was now the boss of many people. Whenever anyone came in, he would pick up the phone and pretend to have a conversation with someone important to show off his exalted position. One day, seeing two people come into his office, the Colonel picked up the phone and said, ‘Hello, is this the President of the United States? I'm Colonel Madhavan calling from India. What is the news there? Hope your wife and children are doing well. Please convey my regards to them.' He went on and on for a long time before hanging up. Then he turned to the visitors, who were patiently waiting the entire time, and asked them authoritatively, 'Who are you? Why have you come?' The visitors humbly replied, 'We are employees from the telephone company. Since no one has been using this office for the last six months, this phone connection was disconnected. We have come to restore the connection.'

"Look, who became the fool here? Didn't it become public knowledge that this officer had been showing off his importance in front of everyone else, all this while using a phone without a connection! This is the danger that ego causes for us.

"Guru and God are within each of us. But as long as the ego exists one cannot know Him. Ego is the veil that hides the Divine within. If one finds the Guru that is in oneself, then one can see the Guru in any object in the universe. When Amma was able to see the Guru within herself, even a grain of sand that was outside of her became her Guru. Amma's children may think, if that is the case, does Amma consider these stones and thorns as her Guru? Yes, even a thorn is a Guru for Amma. A person walking carelessly down a path started focusing on the path ahead when a thorn pricked his foot. Hence, getting pricked by a thorn helped him, not just to avoid more thorns, but also to notice a cobra lying on the road and to avoid death itself. Amma considers this body also as a Guru. When reflecting on the impermanence of the body, I realize that only the Atman is eternal. Everything around has only led Amma to good. Hence Amma has only reverence for everything in life.

"Amma always says that we should have the attitude of a beginner.

Because only a beginner will have the patience to sit and learn. Even if the body grows big, our mind is not expanding proportionately. In order for the mind to grow and become as big as the universe, we must first have the attitude of a child. Only a child has the potential to grow. Our present attitude is egoistic; it is of the body and mind. Only if we let go of this and adopt the innocence of a child, will we get the ability to pay attention to what others are saying. No matter how much water falls on a mountain top, it will not collect there. Instead, water will flow naturally into a hole from all four sides and fill it up. Like this, if we have the attitude that "I am nothing", whatever we need will find us. Patience and attentiveness are the true earnings in our life. One who gains these will be successful anywhere. Patience and attentiveness are priceless. When patience and attentiveness manifest, the mirror that helps us to recognize and remove inner impurities becomes visible within. One becomes the mirror of his own mind and gains the ability to understand how to remove impurities from one's psyche without anyone else's help. Such people see only a Guru in everything. They cannot see anyone as inferior to them. Those who grew up like that will not engage in unnecessary arguments. They do not live by mere talk. Their life is visible in their actions.

"Ego is like cancer. It will keep destroying us as it grows. We do not usually understand this. And if anyone points this out, we will see them as enemies. That is why it is said that we should rely on a Guru, or a self-realized master. Thus, when a spiritual aspirant relies on the Guru, he realizes that it is his own ego that stands in the way of his self-realization. The Guru brings it out by creating many situations and destroys it. It may sometimes be through love, sometimes through scolding, and many times through other people. In other situations, the Guru may teach the lesson by being humbler than the disciple. Thus, the Guru melts the ice block of ego in us and turns it into pure water, which helps to quench the thirst of others. Thus, it becomes useful for the world and above all for his self-realization."

15. ALERTNESS

"In life, we need the same alertness that we have when we are waiting at a traffic light."

– Amma

Through this example, Amma is explaining that a person who has an awareness of the goal will find an opportunity to achieve that goal in any situation.

When our vehicle is stopped at a traffic light, we have only one goal and that is to cross that light. So, we will wait with alertness for the light to turn green, without looking anywhere else. In order to achieve anything in life, we need a sense of purpose. Those who have this will look for a way to achieve that objective in any situation. When we have a sense of purpose like this, we will always proceed with alertness.

Amma says, "When a student wants to get first rank in an examination, he does not waste any time. Even though he likes movies, he won't watch any movies until the exam is over. No matter how many friends call, he won't go out with them. Towards this end he eats less at night and reduces sleep, giving importance to studies. No matter how many relatives visit his house, he will not waste time chatting with them.

Not only that, even while bathing, brushing his teeth or doing any activity, he will be reflecting on what he has learned. Thus, he will always act and behave with alertness.

"Today most people depend on God only to get their wishes fulfilled. That is not love for God but love for things. Today we have no compassion for anyone because of selfish desires. How can God's grace exist in a heart that has no compassion for others? How can his sorrows disappear? Putting faith in God just for fulfillment of desires will not free one from sorrow. If we want to get rid of sorrows, what we need to pray for is removal of desires, devotion, and faith in the Divine. Then God will fulfill all our needs. It is not the trivial things in the royal palace that we must love - try to love the king himself. If we get hold of the king, we may get access to the entire palace treasury. 'Give me a job, give me a house, give me a child...' this is not how we should pray to God. We should pray, 'O Lord, come, be mine'. Once we gain God and obtain His grace, the three worlds will come under our feet. We will also gain the power to rule these. But first, our actions must be good.

"When we meditate and pray, if we concentrate fully, it is like recharging our spiritual battery. Praying should be for the sake of God alone. Only then can one attain complete contentment in life. Anything that falls into jaggery will become sweet. Similarly, when we are near to God, all that we get is joy. If we catch the queen bee, all the other bees will follow. If we depend on God, spiritual and material achievements will follow.

"For those who trust in God just for fulfillment of their desires, if their desires come true, their devotion and faith in God will increase. If they are not fulfilled, they lose whatever little faith they had. How can God fulfill everyone's wishes? A doctor's prayer is, 'I should get many patients every day.' He always prays to God for this. If he doesn't get patients, won't he lose faith in God? At the same time, the patients' prayer is, 'God, don't make us sick anymore. Please cure us of our diseases.' A lawyer prays to get new cases every day. However, other people pray that they don't get caught in any legal battles. If someone buys a vehicle meant to transport dead bodies, his daily prayer is to get 'a dead body without fail'. The coffin seller's prayer is the same. Meanwhile, what is the prayer of the living? That they should never die. How can the wishes of all these people be fulfilled at the same time? The world is full of contradictions like this. Getting everyone's desires fulfilled equally is difficult. In this world full of contradictions, it is not difficult to live with peace and contentment. It is just enough to understand spiritual principles and live following them.

"It is not difficult for a person who has studied Agriculture to plant and grow a coconut tree. If the coconut is affected by any disease, he can quickly detect it and remedy it. Similarly, if you understand spiritual principles and live your life in accordance with them, you can move forward without getting defeated by any crisis. When you buy a machine, you also get a manual that explains how it works. If you study that you can operate the machine properly. If you run the machine without reading and understanding it, the machine will breakdown soon. Similarly, spiritual books and Mahatmas teach us how to live in this world. If we follow them, life will be successful. If not, the result will be more sorrows due to a self-absorbed life.

"When a student sits in the exam hall, he will be alert throughout the duration of the exam. He knows that God will not increase the time for him. Hence, he will keep trying to finish writing the exam while staying alert every single moment. Only then can he achieve his goal. Similarly, we can achieve the goal of life only if we remain alert like this in our life as well."

16. NEW BRAKES FOR THE MIND

"Angry words spilling out is like an old car that does not stop when we hit the brakes. We have to be like new cars that stop right away. We have to control anger like this, recognizing it as soon as it arises."

- Amma

If you hit the brakes of some cars, like the old Ambassador, while driving at high speed, you do not stop right there. You go on for some distance before the car rolls to a stop. But the new model cars are not like that. They will stop exactly when you hit the brakes, no matter how fast you are going.

An advertisement for Mercedes Benz in the United States goes like this: A Benz car is traveling at a speed of 200 kmph. In the back seat of this car is a beautiful young woman holding a glass full of water. The brakes are suddenly applied in this car going at such a speed. But not even a single drop of water falls out of that glass.

Such is the difference between ordinary people and Mahatmas. The danger that anger engenders in ordinary people is considerable. One's ability to control anger is like having good brakes in your car. How many good lives have been ruined by not forgiving where one should forgive!

Let's see what Amma says on this topic. "Once the manager of a company came and sat for breakfast before leaving for work. While eating, his little child came nearby and knocked a teacup on the table. The tea spilled on the man's shirt and pants as well. He got angry with the child, then called his wife to scold her for not paying attention to the child. When he went to find a new set of clothes, they were not ironed. Again, he called his wife and yelled at her. After all this, when he went to fetch the child to take him to school, the child was sitting down crying. The child had not been helped into his school uniform. As it was time for the wife to go to the office, she left the little one's care with her husband and left. So by the time he calmed the child down and had him put on the uniform, the school bus had already left. So, he got his car and drove the child to school.

"Since they were speeding, because they were running late, he was pulled over by the traffic police and given a hefty fine. Like that, he lost a lot of time. After all this, when he reached school, he was scolded by the principal for reaching so late. Finally, when he reached his office, the chairman of the company was waiting. On that day, there was a very important meeting with a valuable client from abroad. As soon as the chairman saw him arriving late, he scolded him: 'Didn't you know about today's meeting? Didn't we make it clear yesterday that today is a very important meeting for the company? So why have you come in late? Anyway, what is done, is done. Do not repeat this again. Get the files prepared for the meeting quickly. The client is waiting for the meeting to start.' Upon hearing these words, the man remembered that amidst the problems of that morning, he had forgotten to take his briefcase with all those important documents. Suffice it to say that this incident marked the end of his employment with that company.

"See the harm caused by getting angry about a trivial matter! Here, when he spilled the tea, if he could have thought, "The child has no understanding, so shouldn't I be the one to forgive him?" that day could have turned out to be an uplifting one, instead of the downfall in his life. When the splitting of Uranium atoms is controlled, it can provide electricity for an entire city. But, when the splitting of these same atoms is uncontrolled (chain reaction) it can explode as an atomic bomb and destroy an entire city. Anger is like this. We should always remember that it marks the beginning of a 'chain reaction'. In the Ramayana, at the start of building the Sethu (bridge to Lanka), Sage Valmiki describes that Lord Rama 'called forth' his anger when he saw that the God of the ocean was not appearing despite prayers and fasting. This is like supervisors, who often need to 'act' angry, in order to push lazy employees and procrastinators. So, always treat anger as a faithful servant and never become a slave to it.

"That is why Amma says that the purpose of all the spiritual practices is to awaken awareness in every thought, word and deed. A Yogi doing penance in the Himalayas, a housewife working in the kitchen, a soldier fighting on the battlefield, a pilot controlling an airplane - awareness is essential for all of them. A moment's inattention is enough to pave the way for great calamity. The result may lead to grief and misery for oneself and others.

"Today even though we have knowledge, awareness has not happened. People smoke, knowing that smoking cigarettes could cause cancer. However, when they know that they have cancer and that continuing to smoke could cause death, they stop without anyone's encouragement. Like this, a person who never had any discipline with food can be seen carefully following a diet prescribed by a physician, when a serious illness affects him. Most of the time, we are jolted into awareness only when we are in danger. However, if we are mindful of the consequences of each of our actions ahead of time, we can avoid most of the mistakes that happen in life. In this era of information explosion, we all have knowledge at our fingertips. But, to lift this knowledge into awareness, one must proceed carefully, using discernment in each of our actions.

"When we go to a police station, we ordinary people behave very cautiously. Walking, talking or standing, all will be done with much care. Otherwise, we know that it could cause trouble. Similarly, when we go to some countries and don't follow their rules of conduct, we will be sent back to our home country. When we remember our goal of going abroad, we are able to obey their rules very diligently. This attentiveness is there within all of us, we need to awaken this attitude and maintain it constantly.

"In the canteen of a college hostel, it was common for some students to take extra food on their plate, eat only a little, and throw the rest in the trash. Upon hearing this, the hostel warden told them, "There are so many poor people in this world who cannot afford even one meal. There are so many going thirsty desperate for even a drop of drinking water. There are people lying on the floor in hospitals without any mats or blankets. The money spent on wasted food can be used to buy medicine, mats, or blankets for those poor people." There was no change in the students' behavior. Eventually a 'fine' was imposed on those who wasted more than a specified quantity of food. A rule that a certain fine would be imposed for a certain amount of wasted food was instituted. With that, the daily food wastage was reduced from eight buckets to one bucket. Eventually it fell to a quarter bucket. Finally, there was no food wastage. The students became more conscious when they realized they would have to pay a fine; thus, their actions became mindful.

"The world is an open book for one whose awareness has been awakened. Every object in nature is his teacher. In the Srimad Bhagavatam, there is the story of the Avadhuta who searched and found twenty-four Gurus in nature and imbibed lessons from them. If we observe nature with discernment, we can absorb lessons from every object in it. What we consider as trivial could teach us very important lessons. We just have to observe them with patience, discernment and attentiveness.

"A person who has never committed any crime until now, may become a murderer or a robber tomorrow. So, we should always watch our own mind. We should not lose our attention and discernment even for a moment. The more we observe the mind carefully, the more we can identify the good and bad in us. Nothing can be seen in the darkness of night. When it starts getting light in the east, we are able to see the adjacent objects. As the sun keeps rising higher and the light keeps spreading, the objects gain more clarity. Similarly, when we gain more clarity of intelligence through spiritual practice, we will be able to see our faults and shortcomings more clearly. It will become possible to face them with discernment and resolve them.

"Action done with discernment and attention is the true prayer. Every action of a person who lives each moment with awareness is a prayer. There is no need for such people to set aside a special time for prayer. They need not be concerned about success in life or liberation. All success will come find them."

17. NECESSITY AND LUXURY

"While traveling in our car, if we see a bigger, newer, or more expensive car than ours, we may have a desire to own it. But we can't always buy every car we want. Only if we control our desires, by recognizing that we cannot buy and drive many cars all at the same time, can we move forward in life. No one can fulfill all their desires all the time."

- Amma

Through this, Amma conveys the need to control the endless desires in life.

When we travel by car, we see many cars that are more expensive or newer than ours. When we see them, we may feel a desire to own them. But we are able to control that desire because we don't have the money for it.

Like this, we will have many desires in life. We cannot live without desires. But those desires should be for fulfilling the needs of life. The desire for luxury often leads to disappointment. In today's world, we see luxury being given more importance than necessity. We know that many people take loans or borrow money and build big houses. Many of them end up in debt and become miserable; some even commit suicide.

Let us see what Amma says about this, "Only a mind capable of renouncing unnecessary desires is entitled to peace of mind. It's easy to give up things we don't like, but not everything we like may be good for us. For example, if a patient eats food that is not part of his prescribed diet, his illness becomes serious. We should be able to give up unfavorable things and habits. This is possible only if discernment is developed.

"When there is right knowledge, sacrifice happens naturally. What is the source of pleasure one gets when smoking a cigarette? Some people hold their nose because they cannot bear the smell of cigarettes. If everyone found happiness in the cigarette, it would not be like this. Thus, the pleasure is not in the cigarette, it is our liking for it that gives us pleasure and happiness. Realizing this truth can gives us the strength to quit smoking. If a lizard falls into the tea we are about to drink, we will not drink it.

"It is difficult to overcome a craving when the object of our addiction is near us. If a drunkard keeps a bottle of alcohol next to him and vows, 'I won't drink alcohol anymore', his hand will go to the bottle without knowing it, and the liquor will go into his mouth. The story about Bali's boon makes this clear. Bali is the symbol of Desire. He cannot be defeated when fighting face-to-face because Bali gets half the strength of those he fights against. This means that the proximity of the object of desire steals half of our power to overcome the compulsion for it. Moreover, Kama (desire) and Lord Ram can never be together in the same place. That is why Lord Ram killed Bali while hiding. It is possible to overcome material desires only by keeping away from the objects of desire.

"Sacrifice is not difficult for one who has awareness of the goal. When the thought arises to get first rank in an exam, students leave aside all fun and jokes and study hard, with no sleep. It doesn't even feel like a sacrifice to such students. If we have true love for the goal, we can find enjoyment even in the hardship we face to achieve it. A porter may find his load a burden. But a pregnant woman does not view carrying her baby in her belly for nine months as a burden. The difficulties become joyful when she thinks about the child who will be born. Like that, mountaineers climb ten-thousand-foot mountains without gaining anything. It is a pleasure for them. They do not get proper food or sleep. There is not even enough air to breathe properly. They suffer unbearable cold. They see death in front of them. Still, none of these are problems for them when they keep their goal in mind.

“Once a visiting king prostrated before a Sanyasi (ascetic). The Sanyasi asked, ‘What is reason for paying your respects to me?’ The king said, ‘You too were once a king. You renounced your kingdom and all wealth and adopted ascetism. I was honoring that great sacrifice.’ Then the Sanyasi said, ‘You are a much greater renunciate than I am.’ Hearing this, the king asked in surprise, ‘How am I a Mahatyagi (great renunciate)?’ The Sanyasi smiled and said, ‘Take the case of a man who owns a large palace. Can we say that it is a sacrifice if the garbage from cleaning that palace is thrown out?’ ‘Never,’ said the king. The Sanyasi continued, ‘But what if he renounces the palace and lives with the garbage?' The king said, 'Then he is indeed a great renunciate.' Then the Sanyasi said, "If that is the case you are a great renunciate. You have renounced the inner bliss, which is superior to the palace and the kingdom. And you are enjoying the royal pleasures that are equivalent to garbage.' The Sanyasi was not mocking the king, he was making it clear that material wealth is extremely insignificant and short-lived.

"When we understand the insignificance of something, it becomes easy to let go of it. If discernment is applied properly, it will not be difficult for us to identify what needs to be given up in any life situation. This is the right path to success in life.

"That's why Amma says, you can have desires in life. Man cannot live without desires. Liberation is also a desire, but it all needs to be controlled. If we think deeply, we will understand one thing--that hidden behind every sorrow is a desire. Trying to find satisfaction by fulfilling all desires is like trying to put out a fire by pouring ghee, clarified butter, onto it. The more ghee we pour, the more the fire will keep burning."

18. RELEVANCE OF SPIRITUALITY

"Driving, after learning to drive well, will get us to the destination. Otherwise, it will end in an accident. Likewise, if we lead our lives with an understanding of spirituality, we can achieve life's goal."

- Amma

Spirituality is the science and art of living. This should be understood first.

We know that most road accidents happen due to improper handling of the vehicle. The reason is that drivers have not learned how to drive properly. Only if we learn how to drive properly, will we be able to drive well. Only then can road accidents be avoided.

For example, how many drivers today know where not to overtake and pass other vehicles? Only a few people really know this.

We should not overtake on an uphill road, coming down a steep road, on bends, on bridges, on school premises, when processions are approaching, on busy roads, at railway crossings, and at intersections. While overtaking in these places, even if another vehicle comes and hits our car, the blame will be attributed to us. If we understand all this while driving, we can avoid at least some car accidents.

The same thing happens in our journey of life. Our experienced sages have told us how to live properly. That is spiritual science. Spirituality teaches how to live with equanimity, even if there are problems in life.

Let's listen to what Amma says about this:

"Worldly life can be compared to an ocean full of waves. One who has learned to swim moves forward enjoying the waves without drowning in them. But one who has not learned to swim gets caught up in its waves and dies. This is the difference between the life of one who understands spirituality and one who does not.

“Today, we live in a world of hopes and expectations: the hope that the violence and conflict around us will decrease; the hope that the prices of fuel, food items and gold will decrease; the parents’ hope that their children will get ahead; the children’s hope that the quarrels and fights between their parents will cease, and the house will be filled with an atmosphere of love and happiness. In this way, man lives with a hundred expectations today. However, the incidents happening around us every day do not heed our expectations. Everyone's goal is happiness, but no one is getting that either. Moreover, some events unfold in a way that take away even the little happiness we have. The reason for all these circumstances is man’s uncontrollable pride and greed.

"Already, the problems that people face in their personal and social lives have started impacting their physical and mental health. So many new diseases are emerging every day! Man has not been able to discover appropriate medicines or remedies for many of these. Heart disease, diabetes, and high blood pressure affect many when they are still young. Mental stress, and resultant mental illnesses, are increasing suicidal tendencies in young and old alike. The number of young people addicted to drugs is increasing incessantly.

"If man is to regain at least some of the joy and peace he has been losing, the only path left is to adopt a way of life rooted in spirituality. This cannot be delayed any longer. What Amma means by spirituality is to build a life based on faith in Dharma (right actions), the divine power and good deeds. At the same time, we must not run after all the scams that are pretending to be spirituality.

"If we truly desire happiness and peace, we must change our outlook on life. Everyone insists that others should change. That doesn't always happen. First, change yourself. If the transformation in us is genuine, it can inspire others to change. Insisting that others change without changing ourselves is pointless. It is like trying to straighten a dog's tail.

"Once a man approached a doctor and said, 'My wife's hearing seems to be going away. I get a response from her only after repeating something twice or thrice.' The doctor said, 'Do one thing. When you go home today, ask your wife something from twenty feet away. If you don't get an answer, keep moving five feet closer and repeat the question. It will give us an approximate idea how bad her hearing loss is.' Following the doctor's advice, the husband went home and stood twenty feet away and asked his wife, 'What's for dinner today?' He did not hear a response. He repeated the question after moving five feet closer. No reply could be heard. He came a little closer and asked the same question again. After he had done this four times, he heard his wife cry out in an ear-splitting voice, 'Hey man! How many times do I have to say that dinner will be kanji (rice porridge) and payaru (lentils)!'

"We must first be ready to identify and rectify our own shortcomings and mistakes. Only through this can we create a new world filled with happiness and peace. That is why I am saying that we need to understand spirituality first."

19. WHEN HABITS BECOME OUR CHARACTER AND EAT AWAY AT US

"A man is used to keeping his car key on the table. If one day he suddenly starts to keep it in his pocket, he will still go to the table and search for the key for many days, without even realizing it. Similarly, what we do regularly becomes habit, and habit becomes character. If we want to change that, it will take time."

- Amma

That means any practice becomes a habit over time, and that habit becomes our character, and that character consumes us. Whether a repeated action is good or bad, harmful or beneficial, it becomes character over time. It is this character that shapes us.

Let's see what Amma has to say about this: "These days, new

discoveries of modern science have made human life comfortable and easy. Machines and tools suitable for anything and everything are available now, but, with this, the physical and mental powers of man seem to be waning. Despite the increase in wealth and comfort, today's human life is full of unrest, discontent, disappointment, and doubt.

"Amma travels all over the world to rich countries and poor countries. There is no shortage of grief and problems in either place. India has more than 1 billion people, while the population of the United States is only about 300 million. And yet, compared to our country, there are more mental hospitals and mentally disturbed people there. If modern comforts reduce human tension and suffering, why do so many people end up in mental hospitals? The number of prisons abroad is also more than in India. What is the reason for this? The truth is that as wealth and pleasures increase, the mind becomes weaker.

"Today, man has become like a 'block chicken', one raised in controlled environment. Such chickens need a certain temperature and a certain kind of food. If not, they will catch infections, get sick and die. This type of chicken has less resistance to survive adverse conditions than regular country chickens. Such is the condition of man today. Addiction to pleasures weakens the mind and body and brings disease. Much of the tension, anger and disease that are widespread today are of our own making.

"Amma remembers an incident. A man boarded a plane for a long flight. As he sat down in his seat, the air hostess told him, 'This flight has internet.' He was very happy. He took out his laptop and started checking his emails. After a while, the internet stopped working. He immediately got angry. 'Are you trying to trick the passengers?' He turned his anger towards the air hostess. Some of the passengers tried to console him. He remained silent for a short time. Again, he spoke loudly and angrily. He became agitated and started behaving like a mentally ill person. Passengers were fed up with him. It finally got to the point where he had to be injected with sleep-medication by a doctor on the plane.

"Today the human mind has become addicted to air conditioners, fans, mobile phones, computers and the internet. If one of these do not work when required, our mind will get disturbed; mental equilibrium will be lost. Today the human mind is so weak that it cannot bear or survive even the slightest obstacles.

“During Amma’s youth, this village did not have electricity or other modern facilities. Everyone slept well, even in the heat of summer. Today, even rural houses have fans and air conditioning. If there is a power outage, many people in the village are unable to sleep. Even when all these are working, most people are unable to sleep. The human mind has become so disturbed.

"In the past, people did not hesitate to travel any distance on foot. However, people today are used to being in air-conditioned rooms and traveling in air-conditioned cars. They cannot even think of walking a short distance. Housewives used to wash clothes, grind rice, and draw water from the well daily, using their hands. Now things are easier with washing machines, mixers, and grinders. But with these, the body is deprived of exercise, and they become sickly, even when they are still young.

"Unknowingly, we have become addicted to many habits that we do not need. Man’s love of luxury and addictions are increasing without control. Mother is not saying that comforts and conveniences should not be there. Don’t get addicted to them. Use them as needed. Be careful not to slip into a state where they start using us. The comforts and conveniences we use today may not be available tomorrow. We have to train our mind to face such situations with equanimity. That is the benefit of spirituality."

Because bad habits will quickly overpower us, we should not permit our mind to use the objects that cause addiction even once. Take for example an alcoholic. Initially, he may have started drinking by giving in to pressure from a friend. At first, he might say, 'I don't want it; I won't drink; don't force me.' Then the friend says, "Nothing is going to happen if you drink just one day. You can drink without fear. From tomorrow on, if you don't want to, don't drink.' At last, the man gives up saying, "This will make me happy." And so, he gives in. When frequently pressured in this manner, the mind begins to find pleasure in it. Later, even if he doesn't see his friend, when that time of day comes, the mind slowly brings up memories of alcohol. Then without waiting for anyone, he starts buying alcohol with his own money and drinking. Continuing in this way, he starts drinking with borrowed money, even when he does not have his own. When he is no longer able to borrow money, he starts pledging gold and other things in the house, sometimes even selling them, to continue his drinking. In the end, when he can't get any more money, he may even resort to stealing. Not only is he unable to stop drinking, he becomes a slave to it. Thus, his bad habit becomes his character and destroys his life.

Now what if we want to change this bad habit? It won't happen that quickly. As it has become character, it will take several days to be free from it. For that, we must first stay away from external circumstances that remind us of our habit. It cannot be overcome while keeping a bottle of alcohol close at hand. When we see it, our power to resist will disappear. If we want to get rid of any evil habit, we must first step away from it externally. We should constantly try to keep away from it. Even if our efforts fail sometimes, we should not just lie there discouraged, but keep trying again. God loves the person who keeps striving for the goal, more than the person who has achieved it.

20. THE SUBTLE INTRICACIES OF KARMA

"No matter how carefully we drive our vehicle, sometimes it may be hit by a careless, drunk, or sleeping driver. Similarly, no matter how careful we are in life, the carelessness of others will affect our life."

- Amma

We must understand that our life does not depend on us alone. The nature of the world is that, no matter how careful we are, the carelessness of others affects our lives also.

We see, hear, and read about road accidents every day in the newspaper. During our journeys, we may have seen oncoming vehicles, or those traveling alongside us, cause accidents due to carelessness and drunk driving. Sometimes, we also have such experiences. At such times, we may have asked God, "God, I have not done anything wrong! Why has this accident happened to me?" But there is no point blaming God for human mistakes.

Amma's words will make this clearer. Let's listen to her: "Many people ask Amma, 'Some people are healthy, some are chronically ill, some are poor, some are rich. Does God show partiality?' Amma says, 'It's not God's fault. It's ours.' We know how big tomatoes used to be, but today they have doubled in size. The reason - discoveries by scientists. Amma doesn't deny that science has many benefits. But while the tomato doubled in size, its benefits decreased. Mothers know that adding baking soda to idli batter will increase the size of the idli (steamed rice cake). But it will not have the quality and taste of normal idlis. Similarly, due to the addition of artificial fertilizers to increase the size of tomatoes, toxins enter our body. Our cells get destroyed. Babies born to those who eat such food regularly become immunodeficient from birth itself. We suffer the consequences of our own misdeeds. There is no use in blaming God. If our actions are pure, the result will be ideal. We are only experiencing the results of our past actions now.

"Once someone entrusted identical stones to two people. One was in good health. The other was thin and weak. After a few days, both were asked to break the stones. Although the healthy man hit it ten times, the stone did not break. But when the weak person struck his twice, the stone split into two pieces. The strong one asked, 'It broke when you hit it only twice. How was this possible?' The second said, "It's because I dropped it many times over the last few days.' Likewise, if some people find life difficult and some find it easy, it is the result of their previous deeds. Our success today is the result of good deeds done yesterday. If we want it to continue tomorrow, we should be ready to do good deeds today. Otherwise we will have to suffer tomorrow. If we show compassion to those who are suffering today, we will not suffer tomorrow. By helping someone out of the pit they had fallen into today, we can prevent our fall tomorrow.

"My children, it is difficult to understand what Prarabdha (Fate) is through intellect and logic; it can only be known through experience. There are certain unique Dasha Sandhi periods (astrological transition periods). Difficulties arising during these periods can vary from chronic illnesses to accidents, unnatural death to conflicts and loss of money. All these can arise during this time. There is no point blaming fate. It can be overcome with effort and dedication. It is possible to make a difference to the Prarabhada through spiritual practices like meditation and mantra japa. Ninety percent can be changed. Amma does not say 100 percent can change because karma is the law of nature. This applies even to Mahatmas (self-realized masters). But there is one difference between them. Nothing affects Mahatmas because they are not attached to anything. In a way, these sorrows are God's blessing because it helps us to remember God. At these times, we can see those who never invoked God even once in their lives, turning to God and the path of Dharma. By treading the spiritual path, one can gain relief from the sufferings resulting from Prarabdha.

"Most people are afraid when they hear the word spirituality. Spirituality does not mean that you should not acquire wealth or give up family life. Please lead a family life and earn wealth, but you should live with an understanding of the principles.

Acquisition of wealth and family life, without understanding spiritual principles, is like buying a comb for a bald head. Neither our possessions nor our relatives last forever. They cannot come with us. They should be given only their due place in life. Instead of asking us to abandon all material things, spiritual principles teach how to live with discernment and happiness in this material world. If a person who does not know how to swim jumps into the sea, the waves will knock him over. His life will be in danger. But one who has learned to swim will enjoy swimming in the waves of the sea. For him it is a blissful play. Similarly, if we understand spirituality, we can enjoy this world even more blissfully.

"Spirituality is not about going to heaven after death or about superstition. Heaven and hell are on this earth. Observing this world as you would a child's antics, can help elevate our mind to the level of experiencing. Spirituality is the principle that teaches us how to gather strength and courage to experience happiness in this very life. Spirituality does not advise us to sit around doing nothing. Laziness is not spirituality. If one works normally for eight hours, it is certainly spiritual if he increases it to ten hours and uses the extra money earned to serve the poor. That is the real worship of God."

Therefore, we must realize that every experience we get is the result of our own karma. God is not capable of mistakes. The result of one person's past actions is not given to another. So, if we try to purify our actions, even if we face troubles from others externally, we can avoid experiencing the sorrow caused by them internally.

21. DIVINE INSURANCE

"Nobody deliberately causes a driving accident just because they have insurance. Even if we get some insurance money, we will be the ones having to stay in the hospital. Thus, if we live carelessly, thinking we are devotees of God, we alone will have to suffer the consequences."

- Amma

We know that the government makes insurance mandatory for all vehicles. So, if there is a car accident, the insurance company will pay for our car's repair. Similarly, if we have medical insurance, it covers our expenses if we get sick. However, no one makes them selves sick because of this, as it is we who will have to bear that pain.

It is like this that we blame God for the mistakes that we knowingly commit in life, thinking that we have devotion to God. We then blame him for the resulting sorrows.

Amma says, "One must understand spiritual principles if one wants to move forward without caving in to the challenges that life throws at us. Whatever the field of action, the core of action is knowledge. If one does not perform actions in the light of true knowledge, one will have to experience unbearable grief and anguish. Spirituality is the path to true knowledge.

"Karma or human effort is limited. Because the result is in the future, it cannot be predicted. Sorrows and problems will be reduced if we keep in mind the limitation of man, the limitlessness of the cosmic power and our insignificance in front of that power. With this attitude, peace of mind and happiness will increase. Performing actions without this awareness is like filling a tank all day long and then realizing that there was a hole in the tank. At the end of the day, there is not even a drop of water left. It has all flowed out. Such is the result of deeds done without knowledge.

"It is in the light of this knowledge that we must embrace Dharma, mutual understanding, and compassion. Only then can the practical way to perform every action and its gross and subtle aspects be understood.

"There were two beggars in a village. One was blind and the other lame. They were very close friends. They were staying in a shelter in an uninhabited part of a village. As it was difficult for them to travel to other places, they would sit in front of the shelter and beg for alms. Since not many people came there, they did not get many alms. They were struggling and miserable with no means for even one meal a day.

"One day the blind man said to the lame man, 'There is no point in staying here like this. Let's do this. You can't walk, but you can see. I am blind, but I can walk. I will lift you on my shoulder. You just need to tell me the way. Let's go and beg together in the market. There will be a good crowd there. When people see us, they will surely help us.' The lame man agreed to this idea. From that day, the blind man took the lame man on his shoulder and went to beg in the market. They got a lot of money. As their income increased, the love and brotherhood between them gradually disappeared. They quarreled over how to share the money. Both insisted that it was not enough to divide the money equally. Each of them wanted a larger share. Thus, their unity disappeared. They stopped begging together. Both of them went back to their old situation. They ran out of money and were on the verge of starvation. It was the love, sacrifice and compassion between them that had saved both of them. With the loss of mutual understanding, once again it was back to misery and sadness for them.

"It is knowledge that makes all actions virtuous and noble. For example, suppose a person goes to take a loan at a bank, where his best friend is the manager. Even if the person who came is his close friend, the bank manager's dharma is to approve the loan only after proper verification of the documents that he has brought. If he grants a loan without checking the documents properly, just because he is loaning to a friend, the bank manager may have to go to jail in future. Then there will be no friend to help him. The manager should have the discernment that if he forgets his dharma and compromises in the name of love and sympathy, tomorrow, he will be in danger. This is how we should live in the world. We should have love and compassion for everyone in our hearts, but every action we do should be performed with utmost care and discernment. Only then will that action be grounded in dharma.

"An action done carelessly is Adharma. Any action done with complete attention will be established in dharma. Spiritual knowledge is essential to integrate Dharma and compassion.

"Considering ourselves to be a devotee of God, or believer in God, if we fall into a pit by walking carelessly, it is we who will feel the pain. There is no point blaming God. For any action, God will give the appropriate result. If the result is not given according to the action, God will seem biased. If we do wrong and expect to get good results, it will not happen.

Even if we are devotees of God, if we live without knowing anything about moral codes and spiritual matters and do not put them into practice in our life, we may not have peace and tranquility. Guru and the scriptures say that we ourselves have to create the peace that we are seeking. That is why Lord Krishna says in Srimad Bhagavad Gita,

uddhared ātmanātmānaṁ nātmānam avasādayet
ātmaiva hyātmano bandhur ātmaiva ripur ātmanaḥ

(Gita 6-5)

One must elevate oneself; one must not debase oneself. Because one is one's own friend, and one's own enemy.

A devotee may have lofty ideals in his mind. It is not enough to confine them to the intellect. They should be practiced in life. Only if there is self-effort will our devotion be fruitful.

Faith in the Guru means living according to what the Guru says. There is no point in blaming the Guru for the dangers that come to us by living according to our own likes and dislikes.

22. IMPORTANCE OF A PERFECT GURU

"The difference between learning under the guidance of a perfect Guru and doing spiritual practices on one's own, is like the difference between traveling in a super-fast bus versus a normal bus. The person moving on his own wanders around and takes a long time to reach the goal."

- Amma

We know that when we travel on an ordinary bus, especially in Kerala, it will go on long-winding route. It will stop at every bus stop and wait for passenger who are coming from far away before it finally drops us off at our destination. But a super-fast bus is not like that. It has limited stops. It also has permission to drive as fast as possible. If we board such a bus, we will reach our destination on time.

Such is the difference between faith in a perfect Guru and mere scriptural knowledge of the path. If we try to move forward depending only on book-knowledge, we may lose our way in many places. It is also possible that we will not reach the destination at all. But when we move forward depending on a true Guru, we will reach our goal no matter what difficulties come our way.

Let's see what Amma has to say on this matter:

"If anger or pride is hidden somewhere in the disciple, it is the duty of the Guru to bring it out and destroy it. The maturity that a disciple gains from long practice of spiritual austerities can be achieved within a short time under a Guru's guidance. Whenever the Guru assigns an activity to the disciple, no matter how easy or difficult, the only goal is to destroy the ego of the disciple and make him fit for self-realization. The disciple needs the Guru's certificate. To get that, it is the disciple's duty to obey the Guru's every word. Like the hammer in the hands of the blacksmith, the disciple must become an instrument in the hands of the Guru. Any command from the Guru should be accepted. The Guru has the authority to make the disciple do anything. Only by surrendering to this can the disciple attain spiritual progress.

"In one Gurukula (monastery), the Guru gave saffron robes (sannyasa initiation) to all but one disciple. The disciple who did not get the robes became angry and upset with the Guru saying, "This Guru is biased. He gave saffron robes to everyone. He gave it to those who came after me. He did not give it to me alone. He is not a Sadguru at all. It is better not to stay here but go somewhere else." The disciple started thinking like this. He started finding fault with the Guru and did not hesitate telling others either.

"Meanwhile, the Guru decided to perform a Yajna ceremony. The necessary items were kept in a house near the Gurukula. The Guru sent the disciple who would not be given robes to that house to bring the items. The woman who lived there gave him the items. The same disciple was sent to bring the items the next day too. Only that disciple was sent continuously to bring things. After regularly meeting that woman, the disciple felt a special attraction towards her. Even after reaching the Ashram, the image of the woman was not disappearing from the disciple's mind. After the Yajna also, the Guru would send the disciple to that house daily with some need or the other. As the days went by, the disciple's attraction towards the lady also increased. It became impossible not to see her. One day the disciple told her about his desire to live with her.

"She made a lot of demands. She agreed to consent to his wish if he could fulfill her conditions. Even though the things she was asking him to do were illegal, the disciple had no difficulty in agreeing to them. Finally, the woman said, 'You have to carry me and walk.' The disciple agreed to that also and went forward to pick her up. Suddenly, she picked up a stick lying nearby and gave him a good thrashing. The disciple ran away. The Guru who understood everything, said to the disciple, who had come running back to the Gurukula, 'My son, do you now realize why I did not give you initiation into sannyasa? It was not out of dislike for you. It is because of this tendency in you that you were not given the saffron robes. The negative tendencies are not completely gone in you. If you are given sannyasa and sent into the world, you would only deceive the world.' Understanding his mistakes, the disciple prostrated at the Guru's feet. All these situations were created by the Guru himself to bring out and eliminate the disciple's negative tendencies.

"Once a student failed four or five times in every grade and finally reached 10th grade. He was pretty sure he wouldn't pass even if he sat for the examinations ten times out of ten. However, his class teacher decided to somehow make him pass that year. He started coaching him day and night without rest. He was especially careful not to let the student get distracted from his studies. Finally, the exam drew near. The student took the test. He passed in his first attempt. The Guru is like this teacher who helped him pass at the very first attempt, while everyone else said that he would fail even if he took the test ten times. It is difficult to attain the spiritual goal even after a thousand births, but with the help of the Guru, the disciple attains it in one birth.

"In every stone there is a dormant sculpture. The sculpture becomes evident when the sculptor carves away the unwanted parts of the stone. Similarly, the Guru brings out the essence of the disciple by removing his inner negativities. Caught in delusion, we have forgotten our true self. For as long as we are unable to wake ourselves up from this stupor, we need an external Guru. He will remove our amnesia. Say we studied hard for the test. Reaching the exam hall, we forget everything in the panic of seeing the question paper. We cannot even remember what we memorized. At that time a student sitting nearby tells us the first line of the answer. Then, suddenly the rest of the lines come back to mind, and we are able to write all the answers without any mistakes. Likewise, self-knowledge is within us, but it stays hidden. Words of the Guru have the power to awaken it.

"When the disciple does Sadhana in the Guru's presence, the disciple's identification with the unreal disappears, and his real essence starts becoming visible. When the sculpture covered by wax is brought near the fire, the wax melts, and the sculpture within reveals itself. One cannot deny the need for a Guru just because there were a rare few who realized the Truth without a Guru.

"God and Guru exist in seed form. But that seed will grow and bear fruit only if the weather is favorable. It may not grow anywhere. Guru is one who creates these favorable circumstances and the appropriate climate. Apples grow in abundance in Kashmir. The climate there is suitable for this. Apples can be cultivated in Kerala as well, but proper care has to be given. Most will not grow. Many will wilt and die. Even if it does grow, it will not bear enough fruit because Kerala does not have the right climate for it. Just as the climate of Kashmir is for apples, the Guru is the person who creates the circumstances for the disciple to realize his true nature and provides the favorable environment to awaken the Guru within.

"Spirituality, like material matters, must be embraced in a practical way. Initially, the mother helps the child hold the cup of milk and puts his clothes on. Afterwards, he learns to do these things by himself. Likewise, help is needed for anything until we are capable of doing it by ourselves.

"People who travel only by looking at a map sometimes wander without finding their way. But if there is a guide, one does not lose the way. Thus, the spiritual journey becomes easy if we always have someone who knows the way with us. Even if the Supreme Truth is within us all, the Guru is required as long as we are identified with the physical body. Once this identification with delusion is let go, nothing else is required. The Guru - God - has manifested in him."

23. WHEN WE TURN INWARDS

"In the old days, cars did not have a reverse gear. It was invented later when the need for it was realized. Similarly, the human mind and intellect are all turned outwards. Spirituality is the science of turning them inwards."

- Amma

A smooth course of life requires an inward focus just as much as an outward focus. Just as we try to change external circumstances, we must also try to change our inner mental state. This is what Amma is saying through this example.

Imagine a motor vehicle without a reverse gear. How difficult it would be to drive that vehicle in crowded places! It would be impossible to back the car into a spot or to park it neatly. Living only for external comforts is like this. No matter how many comforts there are, none can provide lasting satisfaction. For that we have to be inward-looking. Spirituality provides this training.

That is why the Gurukulas of old days provided only few external comforts, and the Guru raised the disciples providing only necessities. The mind that is accustomed to external pleasures does not turn introspective. Meditation and chanting will be difficult with such a mind. That is why the Guru says to give up external comforts. But if there is no pre-acquired tendency, the disciple cannot fully imbibe this. Then the disciple complains, "I can't control my mind, I don't have peace of mind." The Guru's every action and teaching is aimed to help this understanding dawn in the disciple.

Amma explains it like this: "Once a disciple said to the Guru, 'When I sit down to meditate, the thoughts are not leaving my mind. Therefore, I cannot meditate properly, and I have no peace of mind.' Then the Guru said, 'Let go of those thoughts. Why are you clinging to them?' The disciple replied, 'Master, I tried. But I can't.' The Guru said, 'You must understand their nature and cultivate detachment. Only then will it go away.'

"The Guru taught the disciple a lesson to make him understand this. It was like this. One day the Guru climbed a thorny tree in the Ashram with great difficulty. He hugged it and started crying loudly, 'I am in pain! My body is bleeding. The whole body is in pain! Oh, someone come and save me... save me!' Hearing this, the disciple came running. He saw the Guru hugging the tree tightly and said, 'Master, why are you crying like this? Let go of your grip and come down.' The Guru said, 'No matter how hard I try, this tree will not let go. What can I do? Don't just stand there, come and save me!' The disciple asked, 'Aren't you the one who is holding on to it? Why can't you let go of your grip? Then you will understand that the tree is not holding you.' So, the Guru came down from the tree and said, 'Isn't this what you are always telling me, 'Master, I can't let go of these thoughts, I can't let them go.' That's why I said, 'You are the one holding on to your thoughts. They have not come and grabbed you. You alone can decide to let them go.'

"Today man is most interested in learning about the outer world. Humans are spending billions to learn about what's on the ocean floor, inside the nucleus, and in outer space. At the same time, none of us try to understand the inner universe, which is closest to us.

"Nowadays, everyone loves large screen TVs. But as the screens of TVs are getting bigger, the screen of the mind is getting smaller and smaller. It is our selfishness and pride that narrows the screen of the mind. Man has invented vacuum cleaners that have the power to suck up even the tiniest dirt particle. But many people are not cognizant of the need to remove the dirt that has accumulated in our mind. It is our mind that has the power to make our life beautiful or distorted. Hence, the mind is the first thing we should try to beautify.

"The Gods and Demons have been fighting constantly since time immemorial, but in ancient days they lived in two different worlds. During Lord Rama's era, they both lived on earth in two far apart countries. Lord Rama was in Ayodhya and Ravana was in Lankapuri. As time passed, the Asuras were born into the same family as the gods. The demon Kamsa was Lord Krishna's uncle. Both the Pandavas and Kauravas were born into the same family. But today, the asuras are even closer. They are within our own minds. Only by defeating these enemies within can we achieve true success. These enemies are pride, envy, greed, hatred, etc. We have to prepare for a big battle against them to achieve peace and harmony. This is not an external battle with guns and bombs. It is a battle that must be waged within, using the weapons of love, faith, and sacrifice. There is no bloodshed in this war. Rather, there will only be a flow of love and peace at the battle's end.

"No one can live without tension. There will be tension in many situations in life. But we must avoid unnecessary tension. We see birds flying through the sky. No one can stop them. Similarly, we cannot change many situations that come our way in life. Worrying about them over and over again is like letting the birds flying overhead build a nest on our heads. The mere fact that a boat is on the water does not cause any danger. It is only when the water gets into the boat that things become dangerous. Similarly, we live in the midst of the problems of the world. We must be careful not to let those problems build a nest in our minds. This is what is meant by spirituality. Nowadays, many people with heart problems have "pacemakers" in their heart. Perhaps if they had implanted the "peace maker" in their heart, there would have been no need for a pacemaker. Spirituality is this "peace maker" that we must carry in our hearts.

"If we understand spirituality, we can step back and witness our problems objectively. No one else would have had the kind of crises that happened in Lord Rama's and Lord Krishna's lives. But they saw all those situations in the same way a playwright sees a play he has written. The playwright knows which scenes are full of sadness and which are funny. Similarly, one who knows the nature of the world does not need to weep when suffering comes. They can face everything with a smile. He who knows the nature of the world can step back with the attitude of a witness when experiencing joy and sorrow, honor and dishonor.

"On holidays, many people visit the zoo with their family for fun. Even those who shudder at the sight of a tiny spider love to visit the zoo. When we get there, we are happy to see the wild animals, like lions and tigers, in their cages. We laugh with joy upon hearing their roars because all those animals are in cages. We know there is no need for fear. The laughter will turn into tears, if we put our hands in their cages. Then the animals will be happy, and we will be sad. Visitors can enjoy seeing them because they maintain a safe distance. Similarly, we should strive to look at all situations from a distance.

This ability to step back and look at life's experiences from a distance is called 'sakshi bhava' (attitude of witnessing). Cultivating this attitude is one of the goals of spiritual sadhana. Life often brings more sorrow than happiness. This ability to witness things from a distance will help us to accept joys and sorrows with equanimity and overcome them.

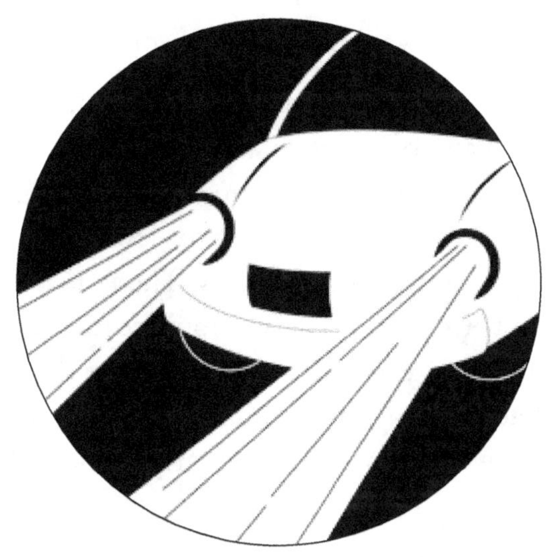

24. THE LIGHT OF DISCERNMENT

"When we drive at night, it is the headlights that keep us from hitting anyone else or being hit ourselves. Similarly, if we are able to see things clearly in the light of discernment, and act accordingly, we can avert most of the problems that we face in life."

- Amma

Through this example, Amma is explaining the need for us to develop discernment. When discernment is awakened, we can see any object as it is and act accordingly.

If we try to drive at night without headlights, it will be impossible. If we drive like that, not only could we hit something, but other vehicles may also hit us. Discernment is like the headlights of a vehicle in our journey of life.

Let's see what Amma says about discernment:

"Amma would say that one without discernment is like a blind person. His vision and perspective will be distorted. He sees only obstacles everywhere. The result is uneasiness and agitation for others as well. Discernment is necessary to view events and people in their due places and act appropriately. Then, no one will need to worry. Doesn't Amma say that we should see an elephant as an elephant and a frog as a frog? Instead, if you see the elephant as a frog, and act accordingly, the result will not be pleasant. What would happen if we decorate a frog to carry the sacred deity of a temple?

"We will regret it if we expect the same service from a nurse as from a doctor. Nurses only have the knowledge and experience of a nurse. They don't have the experience or authority of a doctor. So, they can't act according to our expectations. This is the first thing we need to understand.

"Some people may cry when watching sad movies. They start crying without even realizing it, identifying themselves with the distress and suffering of the characters. But what if the viewer is one with discernment? When we understand that it is a movie, that all the sorrows we are watching are only enacted, that this is just a story, then sorrow will not affect us. Not only that, we can also enjoy the movie. Similarly, if we live after having understood the nature of the world, we can enjoy worldly life as well.

"Many people ask Amma, what is the true dharma of man. Amma says the purpose of human birth is to know oneself. That is, to understand – 'Who am I? What is my true nature?' That is man's ultimate dharma. If not, what is the difference between humans, animals and insects? They too are born, grow, give birth to offspring, and die. But unlike humans, animals do not create new habits and karmic bonds. They live without deviating from their individual dharma and follow the laws of nature. But man? He lives in unhappiness, makes others unhappy, and finally succumbs to death. Thus, we descend to a lower level than animals.

"A Mahatma was talking to someone who had come to see him. The Mahatma asked the visitor, 'What work do you do?' The man replied, 'I work as a clerk in a company.' "What will be your next career move?' the guru asked. 'I will be a senior clerk,' the man replied The Mahatma asked again, 'How about after that?' 'I will be assistant to the Head of the Department.' 'And after that?' 'If I try, I can become the Head of the Department.' The Mahatma said, 'That is great. Then, what is possible after that?' 'If I'm lucky, I'll be the Vice-President of the company.' 'Bravo!' said the Mahatma patting him on the shoulder and congratulating him. After thinking for a while, the Mahatma said, 'So, I was wondering what you would be after that.' At this point, the man's patience began to wear off and he said loudly, 'With luck, effort and a little political influence, I will become the president of the company. Is that enough?' The Mahatma did not let it go at that 'Oho! And after even that?' At this, the man burst out, 'What do you want to know? Do I need to become God?' The Mahatma laughed loudly and said, 'My child, only now did you give the right answer. But you don't have to become God. Even now, you are God. Just having that knowledge is enough. This knowledge is true spirituality.' The limited thought 'I am the body and mind' makes us identify with the body. If one can go beyond that thought, one can know and experience, 'I am the divine power that permeates within and without.'

"Sanatana Dharma teaches us that the creation and creator are not two, but one. There is nothing but divinity here. God is not someone who withdrew after creating the world; the entire universe we experience is God. There is water in the ocean and in the waves. What appears as myriad waves and as the endless and vast ocean is all water. Only the external forms differ. When we see a wooden figure of a horse or an elephant, don't we remember those animals? When we see that form, we forget the wood, and when we see the wood, we forget the form. Such is our current state. We focus only on external appearances. Thus, we forget the indwelling Supreme Being, not knowing or experiencing him. There is divinity in everything. That divine energy is present everywhere. A question may arise, if that is so, is there divine energy in a corpse as well? Even if a bulb breaks, the electricity is not destroyed. It only means that because that instrument is broken, it is not able to let the electricity shine through. Although a corpse cannot let the divine energy shine through, it cannot be said that the all-pervading divine essence is not present in a dead body.

"Pure consciousness has no beginning. It is eternal. That which is changeless is our true nature. This knowledge is spirituality. The realization of this is the goal of human birth. If this awareness is firmly established in the intellect at least, we can, to some extent, achieve the peace and happiness that the world dreams of."

Thus, we must understand the nature of the world. That's why it is said in the Bhagavad Gita - this world is impermanent and full of sorrows. Doesn't Amma say that if we depend only on external objects, we will eventually suffer. That is not to say that we should not rely on them at all. We should understand the nature of the objects and then use them. Today's relative can become tomorrow's enemy. Those we think are our enemies today may turn out to be our benefactors tomorrow. If we depend on one thing thinking that it will give us happiness for life, the result will be sorrow. Don't think that our near and dear ones will be with us forever. At any moment, they, and even I, could die. Doesn't Amma say, when we are in a crowd, we are alone? We are alone when we are alone as well. None of these will always be with us. Therefore, we should try to find an end to sorrow by viewing that unchanging Supreme Being as our ultimate source of support. It is such thinking that should come to us as the light of discernment.

25. BEGINNERS' OVER-ENTHUSIASM

"Just like crowding a bus that can carry only 50 passengers with 150 passengers, in spiritual life too, if you try to reach your goal rapidly, while neglecting the body, the body will become unfit for spiritual practices within a few days."

- Amma

Here, Amma is pointing out the ill-effects of overzealous decisions made by spiritual aspirants when they starts on the spiritual path. Such aspirants often ignore the limitations of their bodies.

Say a new bus can carry about 50 people. Even if 150 people board it, the bus will move, but it won't go on like that for long. Later, the loss due to such overloading will be huge. Similarly, at the beginning of the spiritual life, if the aspirant tries to reach his goal quickly by starving himself, skipping sleep, and performing difficult practices, the body will become unfit for sadhana within a short time.

That is why the Srimad Bhagavad Gita talks about the path of moderation. The food and lifestyle for a beginning spiritual aspirant is taught in the Gita.

> nātyaśhnatastu yogo 'sti na chaikāntam anaśhnataḥ
> na chāti-svapna-śhīlasya jāgrato naiva chārjuna (6:16).

(O Arjuna, one who eats too much, certainly does not have the experience of Yoga. Nor does one who does not eat at all. Neither one who sleeps too much, nor one who is always awake, has the experience of Yoga).

In order for sadhana to be successful, the practitioner has to follow certain rules in food and lifestyle. Neither one who eats too much, nor one who starves himself, will experience Yoga. The food mentioned here is not only that eaten with the mouth. Sound and sight are food for the senses, emotions are food for the mind, and thoughts are food for the intellect. Therefore, like the food eaten through the mouth, that which we consume through the senses, mind, and intellect (our thoughts and feelings) should also be moderate.

One should eat hearty food that is easily prepared to maintain our health, without disturbing others, without harming other living beings. Eating is not just for satisfying the tongue. Amma says to fill, "Half the stomach with food, one quarter with water, and leave one quarter empty." This is how a spiritual aspirant should eat in the initial stages. As for sleep, dullness will affect the person who sleeps too much. It will reduce the sharpness of the mind and intellect. On the other hand, a person who doesn't sleep well will be very tired, with no enthusiasm to do sadhana. A spiritual aspirant should follow an orderly, balanced, and moderate life in the early stages.

The following words of Amma make this clearer:

"A Guru prescribes the sadhana routine we need. It is the Guru who decides whether the focus should be on contemplation, selfless service, yoga, or if just japa (chanting) and prayer is enough for the disciple. Some are not capable of meditating for long periods of time. A small blender cannot run as long as a large grinder. If operated continuously for extended periods of time, it will overheat and burn. The Guru prescribes spiritual practices according to each person's level of physical and mental aptitude.

"The Guru knows the nature of our body and mind better than we do. The Guru gives advice according to each one's level. Without considering all this, if one does sadhana without proper control, based on half-baked knowledge gained from somewhere, it could even lead to insanity. If we meditate too much, the head will become hot. We will lose sleep. The Guru will advise which parts of the body to concentrate on and the time to meditate according to each one's nature. When traveling somewhere, we can reach our destination quickly and safely if we are accompanied by someone who lives there and knows the way. Otherwise, an hour's travel may take ten hours. Even if you have a map in your hand, you might lose your way and wander. Sometimes you may even get trapped in thieves' and pickpockets' hideouts. But if you get someone who knows the way to accompany you, there is nothing to fear. Similarly, a Guru is someone who knows all the spiritual paths.

"Obstacles can occur at any stage of sadhana. During those times it will be difficult to continue sadhana without a Guru. So, the proximity of the Sadhguru is the real Satsang (being with the real truth). Similarly, if one has received initiation from a Sadhguru, one can progress very quickly in sadhana. If you add milk into milk, it will not turn into yogurt. A little yogurt has to be added for that. Such is the mantra initiation obtained from a true Sadhguru. It awakens the spiritual power of the practitioner. If one comes to the spiritual path without knowing such things, and does all sorts of practices ignoring the body, it can create problems. In the end others will say, and you yourself will start feeling, that you are unfit for both spirituality and worldly life. Therefore, in the spiritual path, one should leave aside one's likes and dislikes and do spiritual practices according to the Guru's advice."

26. THE BONDAGE OF ATTACHMENT

"No matter how much you row a tied boat, it will not reach the other shore. Similarly, we will not reach the goal if we do sadhana (spiritual practices) while still attached to relatives and friends."

- Amma

Amma is reminding us that just like a rope binds a boat to the shore, attachment towards anything will bind us to samsara (cycle of birth and death).

One's biggest obstacle on the spiritual path is attachment to various things. First, we must recognize this. Attachment and bondage to our relatives, loved ones, and the things we like are all obstacles on our path. That is why it is said,

"Manah eva manushyanam karanam bandha mokshayoh" Mind is the cause of bondage as well as liberation.

We must first recognize that attachment to our loved ones is a form of bondage. Only then can we be freed from it.

Amma says, "When we are alone, we are alone. When we are in a crowd, we are also alone." There is no guarantee that others will be with us until the end. No matter how many close relationships we have, once we sleep, there is no wife, no children, no yesterday or today. The goal of our life is self-realization, not body-realization. Each person's own happiness is what is most important to him. No one loves anyone more than himself.

Let's see what Amma says.

"A man came to see Amma in the United States. His wife had died a few days before. She was his life. If his wife was not with him, he would stay awake until dawn. He would not eat unless his wife had eaten. If his wife went somewhere, he would wait for her to return. He had that much love for her. But they could not live together for long. His wife began to feel a little sick one day. It quickly turned fatal. She passed away after a week. Many friends and relatives came to the church for the funeral. The body would be buried only after everyone had seen it. The funeral ceremony and prayers went on and on. The man started feeling very hungry. "If only the body could be buried as soon as possible," he said to himself, then he could eat something. He waited for another couple of hours. It didn't look like the burial was going to happen anytime soon. The hunger became unbearable. His patience ran out. He went to the nearest shop, bought some food and ate it. He himself told Amma about this incident. Then he finally said, "Amma, I was ready to sacrifice my very life for the sake of my wife. I loved her so much. But, in the face of hunger, I forgot everything."

"This happened in the United States. Do you want to hear about an incident from India? It was narrated by a woman who came to the Ashram. Her husband died in an accident while riding his bicycle. This woman was his second wife. The first wife had passed away. He had two children from the first wife. When the woman heard that her husband had died, she did not to go to see the body or to bring it home. Instead she went to get the keys to her husband's cupboard. By the time she had taken the keys, people arrived with the dead body. The children of the first wife also arrived. They had come after hearing their father had died, but they also did not go to straight to their father's body. Their first target was the place where their father kept his keys. They knew they had to find them before their stepmother did. Otherwise, she wouldn't give them all their father's money. But the children were a little too late. The second wife had already moved the money.

"Where is the son's love after being raised with so much indulgence? Where is the love of the wife who said she loved him more than life? The moment he died, all eyes were on the property. Children, this is the nature of the world. People only love others for their own selfish satisfaction. Some people are angry enough to kill their wife if they see her talking to another man. When the father falls ill and is on his deathbed, the children are in a hurry to partition the property. If the father has already partitioned it, there are children who won't hesitate to kill their father if they don't get the family home.

"Just because the world is like this, does not mean we should be lazy, and sit idle doing nothing. Give up expectations like, 'My wife, husband and children will always be with me. Even in death, they will be with me.' Know what your own dharma is and learn to live according to it. Do your duties without expectations. Don't expect love, wealth or position. Our actions should be for our self-purification. Let our complete attachment be for God. Only in this can we find joy. If you perform actions based on expectations from others, only sorrow will be your companion. On the other hand, if we live according to spiritual principles, we can experience heaven on earth and after death as well. We can live lives that benefit both us and the world.

"When mothers get old, they say, 'I thought my son would look after me, I thought my daughter would look after me, but now no one is looking after me. They are just wishing to take my money after I die.' We need to know this.

"Once upon a time, a king was ready for vanaprastha (retirement from worldly life). He decided to give all his property to the subjects. He gave whatever each person asked for. A young man came and narrated his woes. The king gave a lot of wealth to the young man. But the young man was not satisfied with all that because when he was going to the palace, his wife told him, 'You should come home only after the getting the maximum that you can get.' Seeing the youth's greed, to make him happy, the king said, 'There is a river here that grows coral. You can own it.' The young man was happy. The king continued, 'But there is a catch. You will be given twelve hours. Whatever distance you can row, while returning back to shore on time, that portion of the river, and all the coral in it, will be yours. But if you are even one second late, you will get nothing.' The young man agreed.

"People flocked on both sides of the river to watch this. His wife and friends advised him that, no matter how hard it was, he should try to own the entire coral-growing river. They also described the benefits of owning such wealth. This charged the young man up. He started rowing. When six hours of rowing were over, due to his greed, he decided to row further. He rowed for two more hours. Only four hours were left to row back to his starting point. The distance covered in eight hours had to be done in that time. He rowed back very fast. His wife and friends cheered and shouted, 'If you are late even by a second, all your efforts will be in vain. Row, Row fast!' The time cutoff time was approaching fast, and the was still a lot of distance to cover! He rowed with all his might. As he rowed and rowed, his chest started to hurt. Still, he didn't stop. He continued rowing with one hand pressed to his chest.

"His fatigue increased. He vomited blood. Yet because of his greed for wealth, he did not stop rowing. The man reached the shore a second before the appointed time. His wife and friends danced, overcome with joy. But the young man collapsed right there and breathed his last. Once the husband was the dead, the dead body had to be taken home. It was very far away, and a vehicle would be needed. The wife said, 'My husband is dead, and we will have to call a vehicle if we want to transport the body. I have children to raise and don't have the money to pay for transportation. Burying it somewhere near here is enough.' The young man's grand aspirations came to an end right there, six feet under the earth. The friends, wife, and children who had urged him to pursue untold wealth did not accompany him.

"This is life, children. People constantly think about relatives and wealth, not allowing their minds to rest even for a moment. They give up food and sleep, not hesitating to do any evil deed, to attain more. But in the end, does anything come with us? No. Right from the start of a desire for material gain, there is sorrow. Even if it is achieved, sorrow is waiting just around the corner because material things are not eternal. They will certainly be lost today or tomorrow. God is the only source of eternal peace. Leading your life knowing that material things are not permanent helps one to avoid sorrow.

"Amma doesn't discourage you from having material wealth or living in the world. But let them be enough for needs; only strive for what is required to live. Understand what is constant, what provides peace, and strive for that. Today, our bond with others creates attachment, and that causes distress. We are distressed because we do not know what is permanent and what is impermanent. Our desires are for what is impermanent. The slow mental agony due to this makes us ill. Our lifespan decreases. Therefore, we need to learn to live in this world, without attachment or bondage."

27. SHOCK-ABSORBER FOR THE MIND

"While we are traveling, if the vehicle falls into a pothole, or hits a stone or a bump in the road, the occupants of the vehicle do not feel the full impact because of the shock absorber. Similarly, if we are able to imbibe spirituality, we can move forward in the journey of life without letting the inevitable sorrows and miseries affect us too much."

- Amma

Through this example, Amma teaches that if we want to see the joys and sorrows in life with equal vision, we need to understand spirituality properly, or rely on a Guru who is knowledgeable about these principles.

Amma continues, "Instead of sinking as low as the netherworld when sorrows come, and jumping high as the sky when happiness comes, both should all be looked at with equanimity."

Amma says, "Spirituality teaches us to understand life deeply. The goal of spiritual life is to live in a way that is useful to the world, based on the realization that the individual and the universe are one. Just as management teaches how to run organizations in the external world, spirituality is the science that teaches 'management' of the mind. Running away from problems is the coward's way. Spirituality is the path of the courageous. True courage is the combination of willpower to face anything, the right perspective, and compassion. That is what you gain from spirituality.

"As soon as a young man takes to the monastic life, there are those who ask, 'Isn't what he did unfair? unrighteous?' Meanwhile, if one's son gets a job and goes to the United States, no one complains saying, "My son went to the United States without looking after me." There is an expectation that the son will earn a lot of money there, so it will not be considered as running away from responsibilities. However, if one chooses a spiritual life, it is immediately interpreted as running away from one's duties. What is the meaning of saying that a renunciate is escaping from life? A renunciate is one who sees the whole world as his home and devotes his life to work for the sake of the world. Amma is not saying that one should leave one's parents for the sake of spirituality, or that one should not fulfill his duty to them. But to interpret spirituality as escaping life is ignorance.

"Spirituality is the knowledge and realization that the source of happiness is within oneself. We believe that happiness lies in external objects. If so, should we not be completely satisfied when we possess them? But even millionaires who own airplanes and ships have anxiety and sadness. While one person smokes and enjoys a cigarette, another coughs and chokes, unable to bear the cigarette smoke. Doesn't this prove that happiness does not lie in material objects? Our urge to acquire things is caused by the attachments that our mind creates. Spirituality is a means of taking control of such a mind back into one's own hands.

"The sea is a nightmare for those who don't know how to swim, but those who have learned to swim are not afraid of the sea at all. Swimming in the sea is an exhilarating experience for them. They will enjoy the swimming even when the huge waves come crashing in. Similarly, if we imbibe spirituality, if we can become the master of the mind, all experiences will be enjoyable. Life will always be a celebration.

"That's why Amma says, scientists may find out that it is possible to construct a building in nature without support pillars. At the push of a button, even this earth may disappear. But none of this will bring peace to one person's mind or a family. Today, we only hear the cries of those who lack peace of mind and cannot sleep even after eating to their fill. Amma has met millions of people over the years. There is one group that does not live peacefully. They are the ones who have everything. If a person is given a job, a beautiful girl, a building or an acre of property, he may not necessarily get peace of mind. Those who have these are the ones we see crying the most. If this is to change, spirituality must be imbibed.

"Amma does not say we must not have wealth or possessions. Earn whatever you need. But it is spirituality that helps us to understand the secret of how to utilize it. Even if he can shoot thousands of arrows together, one who hasn't learned how to aim is only wasting arrows. So, learn how to aim first, then shoot. Then not a single arrow will be wasted. Similarly, once you understand spirituality, no matter how much wealth you acquire, it will benefit both you and the world. If we understand what spirituality is and learn to live accordingly, we will face the ups and downs in life with equanimity."

28. CONTEMPLATING DEATH

"When we are traveling in a vehicle, even when we see someone lying dead on the road from an accident, none of us realize that we too can die at any moment."

- Amma

Although death is always with us, we live wastefully and carelessly because we are not aware of it.

When we travel, we see so many accidents on the way. Sometimes people are seen lying dead after a collision. Do we remember that this can happen to us too at any moment? Even if we remember this, it is only for a little while. That is called smashana vairagyam (momentary detachment). After that, we will continue to drive recklessly and speed as before.

This same truth is reflected in the answer Yudhishtira gives to the

Yaksha in the Mahabharata. In this encounter, the Yaksha asks Yudhishtira, “What is the greatest wonder in the world?” Yudhishthira replies, "Every day, many living beings in the world are dying. Even after seeing this, we think that we will not die. This is the greatest wonder.”

We forget the fact that as we are born, we also give birth to death. For one who is born, it is impossible to avoid death, which follows like a shadow. But many people are afraid to even think of death.

Amma explains this concept to us clearly. Let us listen to her words.

“Once a Brahmin came to King Yudhishtira asking for money for his daughter's wedding. The king who was busy, asked the Brahmin to come the next day. Hearing this, Bhima said to all those present in the palace, ‘Blow the conches, beat the drums, make merry with all kinds of musical instruments!’ The whole palace was filled with noise. Everywhere there was only the sound of beating drums and conch shells. Hearing all this Yudhishtira was amazed, ‘What is this? Usually, it is customary to celebrate like this only when we have conquered other countries. Nothing like that has happened. So why all this celebration?' Those who were present said, ‘Bhima asked us to do this.’ Immediately, Yudhishtira called Bhima and asked him about it. Bhima said, ‘We are celebrating because of the joy that the people and I are feeling.’ Yudhishtira asked, ‘What is the reason for so much happiness?’ Bhima said, ‘I came to know only today that my brother has conquered death. Hence the joy.’

“Yudhishtira did not understand. He looked at Bhima's face in amazement. Bhima said, ‘I heard you ask that Brahmin to come tomorrow to receive alms. There is no guarantee that we will be alive tomorrow. But isn't it because you can keep death away that you were able to tell that Brahmin to come tomorrow with so much confidence?' That is when Yudhishtira realized his mistake and remembered – Death can happen at any moment. What should be done at this moment should be done right now. When we exhale, we cannot be sure that we will be able to inhale again because death is with us in every breath.

"Only one who truly understands what death is, can build a true life. Because, one day it will take away the body that we think of as 'me', all these visible possessions, children and relatives. Whether we fear death or not, as long we remember the truth that it is with us always, we can direct our life to the right path. Thus, we rise to a state beyond life and death. Understanding death helps us learn about life. Everyone strives to make life comfortable. However, one does not succeed because whatever we gain today will be lost some day. And the loss will push us into deep and endless sorrow. But if we remain aware of their transient nature, separation from those things will not make us weak. On the contrary, that awareness will motivate us to rise to the state where we transcend them.

"We need to start this effort right now because there is no guarantee that this body will be alive in the next moment. If we miss the present moment, it is a great loss. If you want to meditate, meditate at this very moment. If an action needs to be done, do it at this very moment. Don't put it off for later. This is the state of mind we need. We must awaken this firm determination. Whether or not we are aware of death, by living a life seeking only external comforts, we are killing every cell in our body. The way of life we have adopted today is harmful to us. Not knowing that it is poison, we accept it with open arms. Every country, every politician and every scientist is striving to increase happiness in life. For that, the intellect has been developed as much as possible. The outer world, whatever can be built up – that has been done as well. But did any of this bring complete happiness or contentment? No! The inner world is becoming more and more dry today.

"Alexander conquered many kingdoms. Still, he constantly felt that it was not enough. Sadly, when he was still a young man, he became bedridden with fever. The disease worsened. Royal doctors gave up hope. Thus, the end of his life drew near. Now, it would be impossible to achieve any of his desires. Moreover, the awareness arose that he couldn't take any of his achievements with him after death. Deciding to make the world understand this fact, he said to his minister, 'When I die, both my hands should be outside of the coffin with the palms open.' The minister asked, 'Why are you telling me to do this?' Alexander replied, "Let people understand the truth that when Emperor Alexander, who conquered so many kingdoms died, he did not take anything from this world with him. That is why I am saying this.'

"In today's society people are busy making money throughout life. That's not to say that we should not make money. We need money to live in society. However, what if earning money is the only goal of life? That is where we have to set a limit. Is it not enough to earn enough for one generation to live? Is it necessary to forget the purpose of this life in the rush to amass enough for future generations as well? We should realize that whatever we earn in this world, the only thing we can take with us when we leave is the virtue of what we have given others."

29. SELF-CONTROL

"Just as it is dangerous when the driver of a vehicle does not know how to stop it, if we are not able to control our mind, it can put our lives in danger."

- Amma

Through this, Amma is teaching us the need to have control over the mind.

What would be the state if someone starting to drive a vehicle without knowing how to stop it? It would be most dangerous to himself and others. In the same way, if we cannot control our mind and redirect it to the right path, our life and the lives of others will be destroyed.

But controlling this mind is not so easy. Arjuna says the same thing to Lord Krishna in the Bhagavad Gita, 'O Lord, you are telling me to control my mind and to be equanimous. But I can't control this ever-restless mind. Attempting to do so feels more difficult than controlling a violent storm.' If such a brave warrior says this, what about us ordinary people? But listen to the Lord's reply, "He who controls his own mind is called courageous." The Lord continues, "It is true that it is not easy to control the mind. Restlessness is undoubtedly its nature. But with long continuous practice and detachment, the mind can be conquered."

Interest in material objects and anxiety about the result of actions cause disturbances in the mind. The Lord himself has said that sannyasa (renunciation) is to give up attachment to these. Mental turbulence must stop. Then the mind becomes controlled. Detachment and the practice of Karma Yoga are the methods for that.

Thinking of the goal without a break is the beginning of the practice. Detachment is knowing that material objects cause attachment in the mind and then choosing to stay away from them.

Meditation is the practice of keeping the mind fixed on the goal, without allowing desires like these to arise, without giving room for other thoughts. Meditation will help cultivate detachment. At the same time, when detachment grows, one will gain more steadiness in the meditation. How we guide our mind will determine our bondage or liberation.

Let's see what Amma says about this topic.

"Like food for the body, the mind needs nourishment in the form of good thoughts. We should know which foods are harmful and which are beneficial. Our diet should be adjusted accordingly. On the contrary, if we get used to eating only bakery products, our body will become weak. In time, we will gradually succumb to various lifestyle diseases Likewise, if negative thoughts increase in the mind, it will weaken the mind. This can lead to physical and mental diseases and, ultimately, our destruction.

"The mind is a stream of thoughts. Without thoughts, there is no mind. If we want to control our mind, we must become aware of our thoughts. We must always be careful about what kind of thoughts we accept and which we reject. A prime minister must have a proper understanding of his ministers. One should know what kind of people they are and how much of their opinions and suggestions should be accepted. If he does something without thinking for himself, and only listens to what they say, he may lose his position. This is similar to the thoughts in our mind. We need to identify them and handle them properly, or they will be the cause of an immense downfall for us.

"Often, we are unaware of thoughts. During rice paddy cultivation, weeds grow. They should be plucked immediately. Otherwise, they will suck up all the fertilizer and destroy the crop of rice. Weeds grow quickly and profusely. We do not need to pay any special attention to them. But the plants that we are growing must be given water and fertilizer at specific times. We must spray insecticides to prevent insects from destroying them. So, it is necessary to nurture them with great care. Similarly, negative thoughts will come of their own accord. For that, no effort is required from our side. But to cultivate good thoughts, conscious effort is required.

"One day a grandfather and his little grandson went to the zoo. There they saw two lions in cages next to each other. The first lion would stand peacefully whenever anyone approached it. Even if someone tried to touch it, it did not get angry. One could see that the lion was very friendly with humans. As for the second lion, it would roar as soon as anyone came close. It would try to reach out and hit them. So, people would get scared and move away. The grandpa asked, “Son! If these two lions fight, which one will win?” The grandson could not answer that question even after thinking about it for a long time. Then, the grandpa answered, "The lion which is fed and nurtured better will win." This is like the thoughts in our mind. Negative thoughts become stronger if they are allowed to grow. Negativities like pride and anger will fill the mind. It will lead us to internal and external failure. Man giving room to negative thoughts in his mind is the root cause of almost all the injustice and violence we see around us today. However, if positive thoughts are encouraged, they will flourish in our mind. Love, compassion, and forgiveness will fill the heart. There will be peace and tranquility in the society.

“Love, compassion, and patience should become our nature. For that we need to remove the weeds like pride, selfishness, likes and dislikes from the garden of our mind. We must consciously watch every thought and dismiss the evil thoughts. Good thoughts should be cultivated. Just as we are troubled when others show anger towards us, not even one person should feel sad because of us. How happy we feel when others behave lovingly towards us. We should be able to give the same happiness to others. If we have this mental outlook, we can respond to any situation in the right manner. The foundation of life itself is love, patience, and discernment. This is what we need today, more than education or money. Everything else can be gained if we have these. Without understanding this truth, people are creating hell on this heaven-like earth. It is our mind that makes this earth heaven or hell. It is us, our mind, that is the light and darkness on our life's journey.

"Our minds have the nature of a housefly. It will go and rest on food and also on feces. But the bee only sees the honey in any flower. The bee does not consider the color, smell, or size of the flower. Thus, if we control our mind, which currently has the nature of a fly, this same mind will become like a bee's mind through the practice of detachment. If we act according to what the Guru says, it will have the ability to always see only divine consciousness in everything. Such a mind becomes the cause of liberation."

30. WHAT IF THE BOAT IS EMPTY?

"A man called out to a boat that was coming towards his own, 'Move away, move away!' However, it kept coming towards him. Not only that, it hit his boat. He got angry and jumped onto the other boat and shouted whatever came to his mind. Only when there was no response did he realize that there was no one on board. It was a boat that had come drifting downstream after becoming untied. Like this, when you gain true knowledge, you will realize that the ego and the sense of 'I', that you had assumed was part of yourself and others, is non-existent."

- Amma

Preconceived notions from past experiences are often the biggest obstacle to giving and receiving love.

Let's see how Amma explains this.

"Once, a man was traveling alone in a boat. He saw another boat coming towards him from the opposite direction. He was afraid that the other boat might go out of control and hit his boat. 'Hey, don't come here! Don't come here!' he shouted, trying his best to steer his boat away from danger. But the oncoming boat kept coming towards him. Finally, it came and bumped his boat lightly. There was no major accident since he had been very careful. But he couldn't control his anger and scolded the second boatman severely. But there was no response from the other side. He got suspicious and looked inside the boat. He didn't see anyone aboard. He inspected it closely. There was no one there.

"It was then that he realized that a boat anchored somewhere had slipped away from its anchor and had drifted, caught in the river's current. He could not help bursting out into laughter at the thought of his own foolishness. He had yelled at someone who was not even there. Like this, when we attain the right knowledge, we realize that our ego, the sense of 'I', is unreal. Life itself becomes filled with blissful laughter. Once the feeling of "I" is gone, we will be able to transcend selfishness and pride, and love everyone.

"Love is the central theme of almost every story and poem in the world. Actually, man's birth and his life are for love. But today, the world's greatest poverty is lack of love. In fact, love should rule man. But today, we are ruled by pride and selfishness. If we observe properly, we will understand that our love today is based on selfishness. So, it cannot be called true love. We see so many people in today's society who marry a girl saying, 'I can't live without you,' offering many dreams and promises. Eventually they abandon her for selfish gains.

"In the western countries, there is a tendency to divorce and remarry if they find a person that they like better. Sometimes these painful separations happen after having two or three children. A love that can disappear at any moment! It is now spreading like an epidemic in our country. How can this be love? Such a fleeting fondness is experienced towards objects. It's like getting rid of the old mobile phone and buying a new one when a new model is released. If personal relationships also begin to be like this, then what is the meaning of human relationships? What is the difference between humans and objects?

"When we understand the Absolute Principle, there is no sense of duality. One cannot see anyone as separate from oneself. One sees others in oneself and oneself in others.

Let me end this chapter by telling a story.

Once upon a time, there was a kingdom called Kashi. One day, they decided to hold a play performance in the royal palace. A five-year-old girl was needed to play the role of the princess in the play. The organizers could not find a suitable girl for this role. So, the queen decided to dress up her five-year-old son as a girl. The prince dressed as a princess looked very beautiful. The queen asked for a portrait of this 'Princess'. The painting was titled "Kashi Rajkumari" (the Princess of Kashi). Fifteen years passed, and the prince was now a young man. While exploring the underground chambers of the palace, he cames across an old painting titled 'The Princess of Kashi'. The beauty of the princess in the painting mesmerized the prince. Noticing the date on the painting, the prince realized that the princess was the same age as him. The prince decided, 'I will only marry this princess.' Her image did not fade from his mind even when he was eating and sleeping. The prince even began to feel that he would die if he did not get her.

“Days passed. Everyone notices the prince's lack of enthusiasm. Finally, one of the ministers approached the prince and inquired, "Prince, what has happened to you?" "I am in love with a girl," replied the prince. "That is very good news," said the minister. The prince said happily, "She is a princess.” The minister said, "Very well. Where did you meet the princess?" "I have never seen her in person," replied the prince. “I only saw a portrait of her.” The minister asked, "Okay, where's the portrait?" The prince said, "It's not a recent portrait of hers. It's a portrait from years ago. But I fell in love as soon as I saw it. I will marry only her.” The prince took the minister to the cellar and showed him the picture. The minister understood things.

The minister said, “Prince, this is not a princess as you think.” The minister then told the prince the story behind the portrait. Here, the minister is sharing the same Self-Knowledge with the prince that the ancient sages of India shared with the world, "Tat tvam asi" – “Thou art that! You are the one dressed as the princess of Kashi." The moment he heard the truth, 'the princess of Kashi’ disappeared from the prince's mind. He realized that there is no girl other than himself. He understood that thinking of the princess and himself as two was ignorance and not the truth. In reality, there never were two separate people. The love and pain of separation that happened, due to not knowing the truth, was merely a delusion. The prince was always the 'Princess of Kashi.' It is the feeling of duality, that the universe is separate from oneself, that leads to desire. As the duality disappeared, so did the prince's desire. This is the essence of Advaita (non-duality).

31. ONE CAN BE BORN IN A TEMPLE, BUT....

"A glider plane is first tied to a vehicle and then towed to increase its speed. Once it gains the required air speed, it is able to lift up into the air because it has been untied from the vehicle. Similarly, we can start with temple worship, but as we get a deeper understanding of the spiritual principles, attachment to temple worship reduces. We can rise to the level of the Self only when we are not tied to temple worship."

- Amma

Only if we are not tied to temple worship can we rise to the level of the Self. An ordinary believer's life begins, and most often ends, with temple worship. Here, it is being made clear that once we recognize the goal of human life and how to realize it,

Atma-tattva (knowledge of the true self) should be imbibed and temple worship left behind.

The glider plane does not have an engine to make it move. It flies using wind power. But to be able to gain enough speed to get air borne, it is first tied and pulled by a vehicle. When the speed increases it is able to fly upwards, only because it is released from the vehicle that pulled it. A lot of people remain bound to temples all their lives. Their lives end without knowing that spirituality and spiritual masters are superior to this.

The goal of human life is God realization. It should be attained by learning the scriptures and by living with self-realized masters. It cannot be attained through mere temple worship alone. Ignorance is the cause of man's bondage to Samsara (cycle of life and rebirth). Only if we recognize and change this, can we rise to the heights of spirituality.

In today's society, the majority of people are temple worshippers. That is good. But if the entire lifespan is spent only in festivities and temple rituals, one does not gain Liberation. In temples today, there is no teaching of scriptural texts, nor is there any effort by the devotees to learn them. Then how will their ignorance be removed? How will their attachment to worldly life disappear? How will the suffering of life dissipate?

Let's see what Amma has to say:

"In ancient India, it was the Gurukula (residential school of a Guru) that educated the youth. Once the children were brought to the gurukula, the Guru took care of all their needs. These children lived in the gurukula as they would in their own homes. They would do all the chores. The king's son and a poor man's son were both equal in the gurukula. This was the lifestyle there.

"In the past they would enter into householder life only after learning the science of spirituality in these gurukulas. As a result, they had self-control in everything. A play is performed on stage without mistakes, only because it has been rehearsed. Even during the householder stage of life, they lived with the goal of Sanyassa (renunication of the world) in mind. After bearing a worthy son for the world, the rest of their life was a journey towards this goal. In today's world, scriptures are taught if you come to an ashram. The Gurus of those ashrams are the ones who teach you how to apply these scriptural studies into life by showing examples from earlier days.

"For example, there is a mantra in the Brihadaranyaka Upanishad, 'Atmanastu kamaya sarvam priyam bhavati'- meaning, 'It is for your own sake that you love everything.' Sage Yajnavalkya is counselling Maitreyi using this mantra. The teaching is like this: 'O Maitreyi, the husband is loved not for his sake but for the wife's own desire. It is not for the wife but for the husband's desire that the wife is loved. The children are loved not for themselves but to satisfy parent's desires. It is not for wealth but for one's own desires that one loves wealth.' So, he concludes saying, 'Definitely, everything is loved not for its own sake but is loved for one's own desires'.

"Children, haven't you seen anglers fishing? The bait is attached to the fishing hook and thrown to the fish. What is the purpose of doing this? Is it to appease the fish's hunger? Is it to fill its stomach? Is it to help the fish grow nicely? No! Then why is this done? It is to catch it, and cook and eat as we like- fried, grilled or in a curry.

"And that's why Amma says that we can start learning spirituality at the temple. Later we can move to an ashram and lead our lives according to the teachings of the gurus. This is how we can achieve the goal of life. Our temple worship today is based on expectation of wish fulfilment. We are happy when we get what we prayed for. If not, we are sad, disappointed, angry. The way we react to the results of our temple prayers with joy or sadness, based on whether they were fulfilled or not, is like young children crying at sunset thinking they have lost the sun, and being happy when the sun rises again in the morning, thinking they got him back. They do not know the truth.

“Sometimes we see people going down the backwaters in small canoes, driving flocks of ducks. There isn’t enough space in that canoe to even fold his legs properly. The boat could sink even if he exhales forcefully. It is that small. When the ducks stray farther, he controls them by noisily striking the oar in the water, still sitting in this canoe. From time to time, he splashes out the water filling in the canoe with one foot. At the same time, he chats with the people on the shore and smokes a cigarette once in a while. Even though he does all these things while sitting in that tiny canoe, his mind is always focused on the oar. If he loses his focus even for a moment, the canoe might sink and so will he. We have to live in this world like this. Abiding by our individual dharma, doing whatever is required, but at the same time always focused on God. In this way, we can attain the goal of human life.

32. THE UNNECESSARY U-TURN

"When driving on a highway, if we take the wrong exit, it is not easy to get back quickly. In the same way it is easy to leave the royal path of spirituality and take the wrong turn. But to return to it, we will have to do a lot of roundabout turns."

- Amma

It is easy to reach our destination when living according to the spiritual teachings of the Guru. But once we stray from the path and start enjoying the worldly life, it will require a lot of roundabout turns to return to the spiritual life, even if we have that desire.

We have seen many people who get on the spiritual path, who then return to worldly life. This happened to them because they did not know how to enjoy the sweetness of spiritual life. Why is spiritual life so distasteful to certain people? It is because of lack the Love for God and detachment to worldly things. If these two qualities are absent, then the sacrifice required for spirituality will feel like a huge burden. Only proper Sadhana (spiritual practices), scripture studies, unshakable faith in the words of the Guru, and love for the Guru can remove this distaste. When there is love for the Guru, there will be a sweetness to any sacrifice. Doesn't Amma say that it is only out of love for her baby that a pregnant woman carries the child for ten months and suffers labor pain. When she sees the face of the baby, all that sacrifice become sweet memories.

For the one with Guru-Bhakti (devotion to Guru) worldly pleasures are like food with bird droppings on them. However tasty a food may be, we would not eat it if bird droppings fell on it. For such a person, as soon as the thought of leaving the spiritual path comes, he thinks, "When I am associated with this body, I have a lot of suffering and limitations. Now if I get married and if my wife gets sick, I will have to bear that sorrow as well. Not just that, if she gets into any scandals, or gets a bad reputation, that also will affect me. I will have to suffer for all of these. What if I have children in that relationship? I will have to help do all that is required for the children. I will have to share in the child's sickness or any disrepute he may cause. And if any of the children are mentally challenged or bedridden for life, I will have to suffer that sadness also. If my wife and I begin to dislike each other, I will have face problems with that as well. If the marriage is loving, I will constantly worry about the pain of separation from her. Thus, the series of sorrows continue without any end." If he thinks like this, will he ever think of leaving the spiritual path?

Now if a person completely submerged in worldly life suddenly wants to give it all up and embrace a spiritual life, abandoning his home and family, will society allow it? When he considers his duties and responsibilities towards his family, his workplace and society, even his own conscience would not agree with him.

"Many people think that ashram life is an escape from the sufferings of life. It is true that some people do become Sanyasis (leave the worldly life), when they do not have the strength to face the unbearable suffering and difficulties that arise. But such people cannot carry on in Sanyassa (ascetic life). Spiritual life is for the strong and brave. There are people who, on an impulse, and without properly evaluating life, leave everything and don the ochre robes of a sanyasi. Their lives will often be full of disappointments.

There was once a husband and a wife. No matter how much money the husband earned and gave the wife, she was never satisfied. She kept scolding him daily. "Not enough, not enough" was the only refrain that the husband heard from his wife. The husband got tired of life itself because of this. Not having the guts to commit suicide, he resolved to become a sanyasi. After traveling far, he found a Guru. Before accepting him as his disciple the Guru asked, "Did you leave the quarrelling at home to become a sanyasi? Or did you start down this path because you are really detached from the world?"

The man replied, "I left my home because I wished to be a Sanyasi."

"Don't you desire anything?"

"No, I don't desire anything,"

"Don't you want glory and wealth?"

“No, I don't want any of those. I don’t have a desire or liking towards anything.”

“Did you come here to become a renunciate?” Like this the Guru asked him many questions and finally accepted him as his disciple and handed him a Kamandalu (small water pot used by sanyasis) and a Yogadandu (small wooden stick).

Many days passed. The two of them set out on a pilgrimage. When the Guru and the disciple felt tired, the rested on a riverbank. The disciple left his kamandalu and yogadandu on the riverbank and got into the river for a bath. When he returned after his bath, the kamandalu was not there. He searched everywhere. He became agitated and filled with the anger and sadness at the loss of his kamandalu. The Guru asked him, “You have no desires for anything. Why are making so much noise over the loss of a kamandalu? Let what is gone be gone. Let us leave". The disciple asked ‘How will I drink water without a kamandalu? I do not have another vessel to drink water with.” The Guru replied, “For you who has no desires at all, why are you carrying around this trivial desire? See everything as God’s will.”

The disciple was very sad. Seeing his sad state, the guru returned his kamandalu. The Guru himself had hidden the kamandalu to test his disciple. Both continued their journey. It was time for lunch. The disciple’s hunger increased. The guru was not giving him any food either. Unable to bear his hunger, the disciple began complaining. The Guru said “Shouldn’t a spiritual seeker have patience and forbearance? Shouldn’t he learn to live without despairing, even if he must starve for one day? What is to be done if you are weak with hunger as soon as it is noon? On the spiritual path, stomach urges should be reduced first.” But, even so, the Guru gave the disciple a powder to quell his hunger. But the disciple couldn't eat it because it was bitter. He started vomiting.

With this the disciple had enough of Sanyasi life. He just wanted to return home somehow. He asked the Guru permission for that. The Guru asked, "What were you thinking when you decided to take up Sanyassa?" The disciple replied, "I didn't think that Sanyassa would be like this. I thought I would just sit somewhere with closed eyes after a bath, mark my forehead with sandalwood paste, then people would come, pay obeisance and give me alms, so I could eat good food in a timely manner. There would be no need to do any work... this is what I thought. It is indeed better to live at home hearing the wife's abuse than to live like this." The disciple quit Sanyassa and returned home. Without developing the right detachment, if we take Sanyassa to escape discord and exact vengeance on others, this is how it will be! "

That is why Amma says, 'Without absolute detachment after properly discerning what is permanent and impermanent, one must not take the resolution to be a spiritual seeker. The one who truly knows all this will never abandon the spiritual path."

33. CHARACTER-BUILDING OF CHILDREN

"Children brought up in the city travel on highways. They are not familiar with the bumpy, rugged roads of the village filled with stones and thorns. In the same way if parents give children all that they wish for, they will not understand when we talk about the hunger or suffering of the common man."

- Amma

In today's times parents raise their children by buying them everything they ask for. They don't create an opportunity for them to learn what sacrifice, compassion, and kindness towards others is. As such, when faced with challenging situations, we see that these children are left helpless, not knowing what to do. Even if we tell them about the sufferings of others, they are not capable of understanding it.

Amma says, "Today's children are raised like broiler chickens. These chickens are given food and water in their cage itself. They eat and grow there. They are not let out of their cage or given the opportunity to peck around the yard for food. They do not develop the ability to tolerate the hot or cold weather outside."

We see a lot of parents in our daily lives who raise their children with so much hardship, without eating, buying clothes, or even buying medicines for themselves. Dear Parents, there is no shame in telling your children about your problems and hardships. Let them also grow up seeing and understanding these hardships. Don't ever think you can make them happy by sacrificing even your basic needs and providing them everything they want. It is not right to keep them unaware of your problems. When providing the children with happiness and comforts that were denied for us, we should remember one thing. It is only when they grow up seeing and understanding the pain and hardships in life, that they will, at least occasionally, be made happier thinking of their many blessings. Only then will they thank God with gratitude for the parents that He has blessed them with.

Let's see how Amma explains this: "Education for living and education for life are two different things. Education for living helps us to earn a living to fill our stomachs. It means going to college and studying to become a doctor or an engineer. This is necessary. But education for life, means absorbing spiritual principles that will guide you through life.

"The goal of education is not just to create a section of people who know the language of machines. The real meaning of education is to acquire a well-developed culture. Spirituality means to live in this world understanding the nature of the mind and the world.

"Once an event was organized celebrating the installation of a supercomputer in a company. The organizer announced to the audience, 'You can ask any question you want. This computer will give an answer.' Apparently, that computer would answer any question within seconds! The audience asked many tough questions on many subjects like Science, History, Geography etc., to the computer. The answers popped up on the screen within seconds. Then, a small child in the audience came forward and asked a question, 'Hello! Supercomputer, how are you? Are you happy?' The computer screen flickered for a while. It had no answer to this question. That supercomputer knew everything about any subject in the world, but it could not answer a question regarding itself. Today most of us are in the same state as this supercomputer. "

That is why Amma says, the values we teach our children are like leaving a footprint on wet cement. That footprint will never disappear. Like that, if the opportunity is provided to grow up imbibing spiritual values in childhood itself, that culture will stay with them, no matter how much they grow.

34. SELF CONFIDENCE

"If a car has not been started for a long time, its battery will lose its charge. Self-confidence is like this. If it is not awakened now and again, our self-confidence will also slowly drain away."

- Amma

Every day we must engage in activities that awakens our self-confidence.

No matter what kind of vehicle, its battery will lose its charge if it is not started for a long time. It is to avoid this that we start the vehicle daily to keep the battery charged. In this same manner, a spiritual person must keep awakening his self-confidence. It has to be wakened and maintained through regular Sadhana (spiritual practices) and Satsang (spiritual discourse, associating with spiritual aspirants).

Amma's words give us more clarity on this subject.

"Once two children went to take bath in a river. One was happily enjoying swimming in the river. While the other one was upset after getting in the water. He kept crying.

"A passerby asked the crying child, 'Why are you not bathing, even after entering the water?' The child replied, 'I am afraid.'

Then he asked the other child, 'Aren't you afraid to swim and play like this?'

That child replied, 'My mother is standing right there. Whatever happens, my mother will save me. Then why should I be afraid?' This confidence in his mother is his own self-confidence.

"Long ago, a young soldier was very afraid of testing his sword fighting skills in tournaments. Seeing him avoid most of the competitions, his friends decided to play a trick on him. They gave him a brand-new sword and convinced him that it had divine powers. They made him believe that wielding this magic sword meant he could never be defeated. The soldier jumped enthusiastically into the arena. He was victorious in every single competition. Nobody had seen such fearlessness ever before in that kingdom. His name became famous. One day, his friends told him that the sword did not really have any magical powers. He stood frozen in shocked horror. In the next competition his knees knocked together in fear. Gasping for breath, his fingers could not even tighten around the sword. He stood there blinking. When he lost confidence in his sword, he lost confidence in himself as well. When he lost his self-confidence, he had to withdraw from the competitive world itself. "

When the path is strewn with dangers, when raging wind and

torrential rain are tearing at our faces, we will have to use all the arrows in our quiver and hold on. To move forward we will have to use all our capabilities. Apart from self-confidence, consistent enthusiasm, courage, discipline, a sense of responsibility, perseverance, honesty, and purity of character will all give us support. We need the love and trust of sincere and good friends. Above all, we need to have faith that the divine power is always with us to help us through any disaster.

Disasters and obstacles are important companions in life. Life becomes comfortable when we learn how to handle them properly. Self-confidence is the most essential requirement to overcome any kind of challenge. The abilities given to us by God are immense. If we don't have confidence in those abilities, we will face defeat everywhere.

Let's contemplate Amma's words again.

"Grieving over the past is like hugging a corpse. We will never get back the past. We don't know the future either. So, children, instead of losing time and peace of mind thinking about those, you should try to make the best use of the present. But today's situation is not like that. We lose the opportunity of the moment by dwelling on things past or things yet to happen. Only God knows about the past, present, and future. And so, children, you must surrender all three to God and try to move forward thinking of Him. When that happens, the smile on our faces will never fade."

"Once a person was thinking while eating an ice cream, 'Yesterday, the fruits in the shop where I ate were all kept uncovered. Could flies or lizards have fallen on them? Was the headache I had this morning a result of that? Oh, this morning my son asked me to get him new clothes again. How can I buy them? Don't I need money too! I have been wanting to build a new house for a long time. My present salary is not enough for anything. Hope I get a better job....' While thinking all this, he finished the ice cream. But he could not even savor its taste. He could have enjoyed its sweet taste if he had focused on the present moment, instead of thinking of the past and future at the same time. So, children, live savoring every moment in life. Either surrender everything to God, or accept everything with a smile on your face, seeing all situations as orchestrated by God. Leave the past and the future and do what is in our hands now with complete awareness.

"If we fall once, we should rectify our mistake and leap forward with enthusiasm. We should think that it happened so that we can develop more awareness and avoid falling again. Whatever happened before should be seen as a 'canceled' check. It is of no use to remember and grieve about that. Looking at a wound and continuing to cry about it is of no help. Timely application of medicine is what is required. No one brings anything when taking birth. He doesn't take anything with him when he leaves. Everything that comes during the interim period, stays for a while and gets lost. That's all! Once we know that their nature is like that, there's no need to be sad and helpless. Peace of mind is the true wealth. We must be careful not to lose it. We must think of a way to keep this."

35. IF IN EXCESS...

"If a vehicle is regularly overloaded, it is harmful for the engine and the tires. Similarly, if we eat food in excess, it is harmful for our stomach and overall health."

- Amma

Amma says that excessive food intake and excessive thinking are the main causes of the present-day lifestyle diseases.

We know that an overloaded vehicle, however new or nice it may be, will experience wear and tear on the tires and engine. Sometimes the tires may even burst. The engine may stop pulling its weight. It is the same in the case of excessive food. If the amount of food intake increases, it will lead to disease. Not just that, the potbelly and obesity from overeating can harm our body and make it difficult to walk.

This is what Amma says on this subject.

"In ancient times, people ate food only twice or thrice a day. But today, many people eat four or five times a day. The reason behind this is that the food today is processed with chemicals to enhance its taste, odor, and color. When we see, smell, or taste such food, the tendency to eat more increases. As a result, we eat too much without even knowing it. The good and bad qualities of food also affect our thoughts and emotions. Each food has its own influence on our behavior. There should be an orderliness even if you eat only Sattvic food (pure vegetarian food). Even though milk and ghee are sattvic foods, remember that 'when taken in excess even Amrit (heavenly food) is poison.' The effect created in our body by each kind of food is different. The mind becomes more restless when we eat meat. It becomes difficult to control our emotions. It is impossible to tame the mind without controlling food.

"Without forgoing the taste of the tongue, it is impossible to get the taste of the heart. It is not possible to definitively say what to eat and what not to eat. With the changes in climate, food's influence on us also keeps changing. What is forbidden here may be beneficial in the Himalayas.

"Stop drinking tea, avoid smoking - some will say these are trivial things. How will the people who cannot control such trivial habits be able to control their minds? And so, these small things are to be controlled first.

"Do not eat to the level of suffocation. Half of the stomach should be for food, a quarter for water and the rest should be for movement of air. The less we eat, the easier the mind control. When we develop pure love for God, it is like a person with a fever. His interest in food decreases naturally. And so, when we sit to have our meal, along with prayers, we should also wish for a compassionate mind. Before we eat, we should remember that there are so many people in the world without the means for even one meal a day. When we remember this, a compassionate attitude will develop in us. Then we will not feel like wasting food or eating more than what is necessary."

That is why Amma says, "If our words and thoughts have to have life and vitality, we must live them".

Once a Mahatma wrote a book on 'Compassion in Life.' He approached a few of his friends for funds to get it published. They all gave the required help. But before the book was given to be published, famine and starvation struck the people in the town where he was living. The Mahatma didn't stop to think. He took the funds meant for publishing the book and bought food for the people. The friends who had donated money for the book did not like this, and asked the Mahatma, "What have you done? How will you get the book published now? Poverty and starvation are common. Birth and death are happening every minute in this world. It was not right on your part to spend such a big amount of money for this cause." The Mahatma just smiled without saying anything.

After many days, he approached his friends again for money to publish the book. They gave him the money reluctantly. But just the day before spending it on publishing, there was a huge flood in that area. Thousands died. This time the Mahatma also helped the disaster affected people by taking the money meant for publishing the book. His benefactors did not like this at all. They spoke angrily with the Mahatma. Hearing all this he only smiled.

Even after all this, the Mahatma somehow collected money with great difficulty and got his book published. But the cover of the book had 'third edition' printed on it. The people who had given money and others asked him angrily, "Hey man, aren't you a Sanyasi? Can you lie like this? How can this be the third edition of the book? Where are the first and second editions? Are you making fools of us?"

The Mahatma replied with a smile, "Yes, this is indeed the third edition of the book. The first edition was when there were famine deaths in this town. The second was when thousands lost their lives and property in the floods. Dear friends, you will gain only bookish knowledge by reading the book. The first two editions of this book showed how compassion can be applied practically to real life. Of what use is a book and words explaining compassion, when a live human is crying for help, and we are unable to lovingly help him up?"

36. THE GURU GPS

"If we have GPS navigation in our vehicle, we must travel following its directions. Only then can we reach our destination without losing our way. Similarly, once we accept a Guru, we can reach our goal only if we live according to the instructions of the Guru".

- Amma

Many of us have GPS in our vehicles. Why? It is to find the correct route to a place we are not familiar with. If we don't follow the route given by the GPS, we will not reach the place we had aimed for when we started.

This example is showing the importance and greatness of a Guru in spiritual life. By 'importance of the Guru,' we mean the significance of the Atma (the Self) that the Guru represents. How does this help us? It benefits us in every way when apply the teachings of the Guru in our lives.

Let's see what Amma has to say about this subject.

"During their school days, though aware of their goal, children's minds are more inclined towards play or other forms of entertainment. Fear of scolding from parents or punishment from teachers is the only reason why many of them study. Once they graduate from school, awareness sets in that they should pursue higher studies, pass with a high rank and so on. Then they study very hard. They will concentrate on studies without anyone having to scold or punish them. They will not go to see movies that much or sleep too much. When they are young, though, they study out of fear of their parents or teachers. This fear is not a weakness. During childhood, we should live obeying parents and teachers. In the same way, when starting on spiritual life a Guru is required to awaken our awareness. Once our inner Guru is awakened then we will gain the ability to function using our own discernment. Until then help from an external Guru is essential.

A Guru's guidance is necessary to know and understand God, who is beyond the mind and the intellect. We should have firm faith in the Guru's words. Some few might have doubts that this is blind faith. It definitely is not. This whole universe subsists on faith. Don't we enter a vehicle only because we have faith that the driver will drive us safely to our destination without causing an accident? Doesn't a father get his daughter married to a young man on the faith that he will take care of her?

Let us take two varieties of hen. The indigenous free-range hens and the artificially raised factory-farm hens. The chicks hatched naturally, receiving the mother hen's warmth, grow up with the strength to withstand nature. They do not require a special enclosure or feed. Sun or rain, nothing is a problem for them. At night they will climb on some tree branch and sleep. But what about the artificially raised variety? They are hatched in an artificial environment. They cannot withstand the forces of nature. They die if exposed to cold. Sun and rain are all problems for it. Similar is the story of those who grow without the guidance of a true Guru. When faced with challenges they become helpless and collapse.

"If a person sincerely yearns to rise spiritually, the Guru will himself come to him. He should have developed a level of detachment. That is all that is needed. If a small child goes to the edge of a pond, the mother shows the danger and guides it away from there. Like this, the Guru will guide and advise the disciple as required, in a timely manner. Though God is everywhere, the Guru's proximity has a special importance. Though air is everywhere, the coolness under the shade of a tree cannot be experienced elsewhere. The breeze that has caressed the leaves provides relief to those of us living in the heat. Similarly, the Guru's closeness will give peace and relief to us living in the heat of worldliness.

"For spiritual progress one must have the attitude of surrender to the Guru. The teacher first holds the index finger of the child who has come to learn the alphabet and writes in the sand. The index finger of the child is in the control of the teacher. If the child, with an egoistic attitude of 'I know everything', refuses to obey the teacher, how will he learn to write the alphabet? When we surrender to a Guru, we must always remember that the Guru is situated at the level of the Supreme-Self and the disciple at the level of the body and mind. The Guru takes care of his disciples just as a mother hen raises her hatchlings by keeping them under her wings. Even the smallest of errors are pointed out and corrected from time to time. Not even an iota of ego will be allowed to grow. Towards this end, the Gurus may behave harshly sometimes.

"When an ironsmith keeps a piece of molten iron heated in his forge on a stone, and forcefully strikes it with his hammer, one might think, 'There is no one as hard-hearted as him anywhere.' But the ironsmith might be thinking only about the new shape that will be produced when he strikes the iron. It is the same with the Guru. The real Gurus are knowers of the truth. If we live according to their teachings, we will most certainly reach God."

37. THE POWERFUL PRESENT

"When we travel in a vehicle, we enjoy the new sights because we are able to forget those that went past. In life also, if we keep remembering the past, the present moment will pass without us being able to enjoy it."

- Amma

If we keep remembering the past, we will not be able to enjoy the present moment. The deep impressions left by past experiences are obstacles that prevent us from giving and receiving true love most of the time.

While driving a vehicle, we see a lot of roadside scenes. But, as our vehicle keeps moving ahead, we don't keep those scenes in mind. Because if we do, we will not be able to pay attention to the obstacles in front of us. Hence, we are able to travel without accidents.

In the journey of life, there may have been many experiences that are hard to forget. But, if we don't try to forget those experiences, it will be difficult for us to plan for the future. When facing the challenges of life, we can overcome them only with courage and presence of mind.

Amma says, "Most often, it is our own ego that harms to us. In these circumstances we need bring forth humility. Children, it is to awaken the good values in us that I am asking you to be humble with others. Humility is not a weakness. When we get angry with others with the attitude of 'I am a big person', or behave egoistically, we are exhausting the power within us. We are losing God's presence in our life. Nobody wishes to be humble. We lack humility because we take pride in something that is an illusion. Our body is nothing, but an object filled with ego and the sense of the 'I'. This body is polluted by ego and negative qualities like anger, lust etc. It is to purify these that I ask for qualities of humility and modesty to be developed. When we behave egoistically, body consciousness increases. To get rid of the ego, we must bow down to others and have the attitude of humility in our behavior towards others.

"Even the cleanest water becomes impure when poured into a dirty bucket. If we mix sour tamarind with sweet milk pudding, we will not be able to taste the pudding. In the same way, when we perform sadhana while maintaining our ego, we will not be able to completely surrender to God or know and experience the results of sadhana. When we reduce the ego through humility and modesty, our good qualities start coming out. We should remember that through sadhana we are expanding our consciousness from the Jivatma (individual) level to the Paramatma (Supreme) level. So, we should take care not to let go of the awareness that God alone is the truth, even for a single moment. When that is so, we will not feel sad and helpless no matter what we may lose externally.

How is Amma able to love every person that comes to Her? Amma knows that the same Self is residing in Her and them. So, she doesn't see anyone as separate from Herself.

"We will not suffer if we live knowing the nature of the world. If are at the temple and know that fireworks will explode, we will not be alarmed. We should learn to live seeing things as our duty, without getting attached, like a bank manager. There are so many employees working under him. He has to take care of all of them. He also has to take care those who come for loans. They come with prepared certificates. If he gets carried away by their smiles and praises and grants them loans without checking the documents properly, he may end up in jail the next day. He is well aware that 'these people only want to get their things done by flattering me'. He is also aware that the money in the bank is not his own. Even then he will not give it away to just anyone. He doesn't get angry at those who seek loans. Also, will not fail to give loans to the deserving. He executes his responsibility dutifully, that's all. And so, he does not have any regrets later on. Similarly, we should be able to perform our duties with enthusiasm and sincerity. We shouldn't give up or become lazy thinking, "none of this will come with us when we die." We should do our actions with awareness and a sense of duty. We should not hate anyone. We should see everything as different faces of God. We should know that all are manifestations of that Absolute Truth.

"If a person gets angry at us and if we get angry back at him, and punish him, it is like poking open an existing wound on his body, which makes it worse. As a result, the infected pus will spurt on us. The foul stench will spread on our body as well. He will become even more egoistical. And we will become more ignorant. At the same time, if we forgive him, it is like applying healing medicine over his wound. It leads us to expansiveness. So, children live by loving and forgiving. All this may seem difficult. But if you try, you will definitely succeed. This is what Amma is saying."

We should not move forward based on our assessment of past experiences alone. Because people and circumstances are forever changing. And so, we should have the mental outlook that understands situations and circumstances, accepting anything that comes our way. This is the path to avoid losing our peace of mind. If we think about it, when we love someone, we are the ones to feel that happiness first. Just imagine how much happiness we can experience if we can love all! Like this, we should love all living beings.

38. ATTITUDE IS IMPORTANT

"When traveling by train one may sometimes transfer from one carriage to another. The person does not change because he does that. He will not reach the destination any sooner either. It is the same when we convert from one religion to another with certain expectations. No changes are going to happen in that individual just by doing that."

- Amma

If one changes from one religion to another with certain expectations, nothing is going to change in that person. There is no point in changing religions without changing one's attitude.

It is common for many of us to move from a crowded train car to a less crowded one. We ourselves have done this many times! Has that changed us in any way? No. Many people are just like this. Even after changing from one religion to another, we do not see any change in them. If one wishes to change, he should try to change his attitude. Only then will his life change. The words of a changed man alone can inspire others to change.

Let's listen to Amma's words...

"Children, our good thoughts and actions can spread light into the lives of many. So, we should try our best to bring happiness and contentment to others with each action. We need not worry about how to make this happen in our day to day lives. It is our mental attitude that determines our thoughts and deeds. If we cultivate the wrong attitude, it is natural for our thoughts and actions also to go wrong. If we are able to develop the right attitude, our thoughts and actions will benefit us and others too.

"Fundamentally, there is good in every person. Even a person who has murdered many people feels love for his own child. But often, due to adverse circumstances, that goodness does not shine through. With the right guidance and favorable circumstances, this goodness within will shine forth.

"A college student strongly desired to become a doctor, but lost his chance by just one mark in the medical entrance test. He felt a lot of disappointment. His mind would not allow him to join any other course of study. After a few days, giving in to his parents' insistence, he applied for a bank job. He got the job at the bank. Even after he started working, the disappointment of not being able to become a doctor tormented him. He was unable to be friendly to his clients. He couldn't even look at them with a smile. A friend who understood his mental state took him to meet his Guru. He openly disclosed his problems to the Guru, 'My mind is not in my control. I lose my temper even for the most trivial reasons. I am not able to deal politely with those who come to the bank. In this state, I don't think I can continue working there. What can I do?'

"Consoling him, the Guru said, 'Son, how would you deal with a client sent to you by your best friend?' 'I would happily serve him and fulfill all his needs,' the young man replied. 'And, what if I send somebody to you, how would you treat that person?' the Guru asked. 'I would happily welcome him. I would take care to ensure he does not face any difficult,'" he replied. The Guru continued, 'What if I myself come to you looking for help? Would it feel like a burden to you?' 'Never,' the college student replied. 'My happiness would be to serve you to the best of my ability.' The Guru said, 'If that is the case, from now on, believe that every client approaching you is me or someone sent to you by God himself. Then treat the job at the bank as God's gift, as an opportunity to serve. If you can have this perspective, you will be able to deal with them lovingly and experience work-satisfaction as well.'

"From that day on, there was a great transformation in that young man. Once he started seeing God in each of his clients, his work became an offering to God. Despair left him. His heart became filled with happiness and contentment. His colleagues and clients were also equally happy.

"Bhakti (devotion) is very helpful for developing the right attitude in life. As far as a devotee is concerned, God is the central point of his life. When he is able to perform all actions as offerings to God, it benefits not just him, but the entire society as well.

"The company of Mahatmas, devotion, and faith in God each has an important place in developing goodness in individuals and transforming them. When awareness dawns that the same God shines in oneself and others, the sadness and other impurities in the mind will vanish, and love and positivity will shine there thenceforth.

"The essence of all religions is one. Their goal is to purify the mind of man. Love all fellow creatures by giving up selfishness, developing compassion, awakening the divine within, surrendering the ego to the Supreme Self and raising yourself to the universal consciousness-- this is the essence of all religions. The founding prophets of all religions realized this goal in their own lives. But their followers were often not able to imbibe this essential principle. They got distracted by the superficial levels of religion. As a result, religion ended up with both a creative and a destructive face. This is how religions, which should be spreading peace and love in the world, have become the torchbearers of conflict and war. If we are prepared to imbibe the essence of religion, without losing ourselves in the external rituals and practices, religions can certainly lead the way to world peace.

"It is not that rituals are not necessary. They have their own importance, definitely. Ordinary people can progress through ritualistic practices, but we should understand that these practices are only a means to help achieve the real goal of religion. Most people use vehicles to go to their workplace and to return home. But only if we can exit these vehicles as easily as we got into them, will we be able enter into our workplace or home. Religious rituals and practices are like this vehicle. They can take us towards the real essence of religion, but we should stop holding them tightly after they have served their purpose. Beyond the external forms of religion, we should give more importance to the ideals and the goal that they teach. Religion is for mankind. Man is not meant to live for the sake of religion. We should never forget this truth."

Many of the rules and regulations enforced by religion were based on the needs of the times. When we approach the problems of today, we should be ready to reexamine them and adopt changes that are appropriate for the present time. No founder of a religion or Mahatma has ever said that love and tolerance should be shown only to those who believe in their own religion. These are universal values. The need of the present times is to guide mankind to imbibe the real essence of religion.

39. RITUALS AND THEIR PLACE

"Let's imagine that we need to cross a river to reach our destination. After we take a boat and reach the other bank, we should be ready to leave the boat and move forward. Only then can we reach our destination. Similarly, we have to reach the true principle of religion using ritualistic practices, but not stay holding onto them after they have served their purpose."

- Amma

Through this example Amma is showing us where to place ritualistic practices in our life and what the true principle of religion is.

Sometimes during our travels, we have had to take a boat. We do not continue to sit in the boat once we reach the other bank; we leave it and go to our destination. Similarly, each ritual should help us to remember God. But now rituals are becoming mere ceremonies. We forget the real reason why we do these rituals. Speaking of this, a story Amma once told comes to mind.

"There once lived a temple priest. While performing puja at his house, the house cat would regularly come and disturb him. One day, to put a stop to this, he caught the cat and put it under a basket. He let it out after the puja. This became a habit. He would put the cat under the basket even before the puja started. Most days, it was his son who would help him do this. Not long after, the elderly priest passed away, and the puja became the son's responsibility. He also never forgot to catch the cat and put him under a basket before the puja. Not much time passed before the cat also died.

"The next day when the time for puja arrived, the son was upset. How could he start the puja? There was no cat to put under the basket! Quickly he ran to his neighbor's house. He caught their cat, brought him home, put the basket over him, and started the puja. Later, he bought a cat of his own just for the puja because it was difficult to bring the neighbor's cat on time every day. He did not know why his father had put the cat under a basket. He never enquired. He just copied what his father had done. We should not be like that. We should try to understand the principle behind every ritual. We should be ready to practice them only after knowing the principle. Only then can we get the true benefit of the rituals. Otherwise, they will become mere superficial ceremonies."

"Today, people are willing to die for religion. But people are not willing to learn what that religion teaches. They are not willing to live according to those teachings.

"Religion is the belief that leads us to know and experience that each one of us is God's form. The goal of Sanatana Dharma is to guide mankind towards God realization, to raise him to the level of God consciousness. At present, the lake of our mind is turbulent with the giant ripples of our thoughts. Discovering the motionless substratum beneath these waves is the philosophy at the core of religion. This is the theme of Advaita (non-duality) philosophy, that is the focal point of Sanatana Dharma. The great declaration of the sages "Aham Brahmasmi" (I am Brahman, the supreme consciousness) was proclaimed from an experience of Advaita, or Self-realization.

"We normally say, 'I am a Hindu', 'I am a Christian', 'I am a Muslim', 'I am a doctor' or 'I am an engineer.' The omnipresent 'I' that exists equally in all of these does not have a name or form. It is this very supreme principle that is called the Self, Brahman, or God. The world is enveloped in darkness today. Amma is pained when she sees all that is happening. What we witness all around is man running after worldly pleasures and falling down completely exhausted. Man is violating the warning signs set in place by Nature. Amma is not telling you not to enjoy worldly pleasures, but we should all understand a truth. The joy that you gain from sensory pleasures and worldly objects is just a small reflection of the infinite happiness that is gained by experiencing the Self. Happiness is our true nature. We can never gain real happiness from external sources. In the same way that today's newspaper becomes tomorrow's wastepaper, the objects that give us joy today may become the reason for our sorrow and despair tomorrow. Religion teaches us to understand this truth and to live in the world with proper discernment."

"No matter where we live, when we live or how we live, when the time comes, death will take us. In one stroke, it will defeat us by taking away all that is ours. We will have to leave, abandoning everything. Nothing that we earned, no one we consider our relatives will come to our rescue. And so, religion teaches us, 'The goal of this life is not just to nourish and protect this body. It is to rise to the completeness of the Supreme Self that is your true nature.'"

"The one who lives understanding the impermanent nature of the world can live happily without feeling helpless or losing his courage when faced with challenges. It is difficult for a person to face the waves of the ocean if he doesn't know how to swim. The strong waves can drown him. On the other hand, for one who knows how to swim, it is a joyful experience to play in the waves. The waves cannot conquer him. In the same way, for the one who lives knowing the impermanent nature of worldly pleasures, life's contradictions are experienced as an enjoyable game. He smiles and welcomes the favorable and unfavorable experiences of life with equanimity. But for the one who has not understood this principle, life becomes an unbearable burden, ever filled with sorrow. Religion gives us the strength and courage to face life's challenges with equanimity and peace. It builds the way for man to live life happily with self-confidence and enthusiasm. For one who lives imbibing the ideals of religion, life becomes joyful like an innocent child's play.

40. REMAIN A WITNESS

"On a road with red soil, vehicles that travel at high speed raise a lot of dust. If we are behind these vehicles, we will be bathed in dust. So, when we see a vehicle coming, we have to stay far away. Similarly, we must witness our thoughts from afar. If we go near to them, they may affect us without our knowledge. If we watch from a distance., we can see the thoughts rise and disappear, just as we see the dust swirling up and then settling down."

- Amma

We should watch our thoughts from afar. They may affect us without us even knowing it if we get too close. Just as we can see the dust rise and settle on the road when we watch from a distance, we can see the thoughts rise and fade in our minds.

When we go on a dusty road, when a vehicle comes, it passes by raising clouds of dust. We don't walk close to that vehicle during this time. Because we know that if we go near that vehicle, we will get completely covered in dust. That is why we stay away. In the same manner, when thoughts arise, we must practice distancing ourselves from them. If not, we will also be engulfed by the dust of our thoughts. We should always watch our minds.

Amma says,

"Many thoughts together make the mind. They are like the waves in the ocean. They keep coming one after the other. We cannot make them stop by using force. But the waves stop automatically where the sea is deeper. So instead of trying to control the thoughts, concentrate on a single thought. Then, the depth of the ocean, that is the mind, increases. It calms down. Don't worry about getting bad thoughts. The mind is the nest of all kinds of thoughts. Assume that these thoughts arise only to fade away. We should not get attached to them."

"When we travel in a bus, we see so many nice things- lovely houses, beautiful gardens, huge shopping malls. But we don't get attached to them. We see them and keep going because they are not our destination. We should be able to see the thoughts that pass through our mind in the same way. Witness them, but don't get attached. That is what is required. We should not get stuck to them. We can watch the river current flowing; there is enjoyment in that. But if we wade into it, we will be helpless. We should practice being a witness when thoughts pass through our mind. That will give strength to our mind."

"In the same way a pendulum of a clock moves from side to side, the mind moves constantly from happiness to sorrow and from sorrow to happiness. When the pendulum moves to one side, it is picking up momentum to go back to the other side. In the same way we should think, when the mind is going into happiness, it is gaining the strength to go back to sadness, and when it is in sadness, it is preparing to move back to happiness. It is only when the pendulum of the mind stops moving that we experience true peace of mind. A calm mind is the source of happiness. That unmoving state is the essence of life."

"Meditation and spirituality are necessary components in life. To bring subtlety and clarity to man's thoughts and actions, a meditative mind and spiritual outlook are required. Viewing spirituality as separate from life is ignorance. Just like eating and sleeping are necessary for the body, spiritual awareness is essential for a healthy mind."

"Two friends met each other on the road. One of them asked the other, 'Hi, how are you?' 'I am fine,' the other replied. The first friend asked 'What is your son doing? Has he not got a job yet?' His friend replied, 'He hasn't got a job yet. Maybe that is why he has started meditating.' 'Meditation, what is that?' his friend asked. 'Oh, I don't know,' the man replied, 'But I heard that it is better than sitting and doing nothing.' Even now many people believe that spirituality is for those who have nothing else to do. Spirituality is the core of Indian culture. If we can accept the essence of this culture in the right manner, we will find solutions to many personal and societal problems. But today man uses devious means, to the extent that he can, to find solutions to life's problems."

Once a person entangled in a court case was afraid that he might lose. Seeing no other way out, he told his lawyer, "I am going to bribe the judge with an expensive gift." The lawyer was shocked.

He told him, "This judge is proud of his honesty. You cannot influence him by offering a bribe. If you try bribing him, it will turn him against us."

In the end, he won the case. After that the man invited his lawyer to celebrate. In middle of a conversation, the lawyer said, "If I had bribed the judge like you requested, we would have surely lost the case." The man replied, "That's not how it happened. I did send that gift to the judge, but it was in our opponent's name!" This is how many people's minds function in today's world.

And that's why Amma is saying, when unnecessary thoughts come to our mind, we must train ourselves to watch them from a distance. When that happens, those thoughts will subside on their own, and we can find the right solution to the problem in front of us with a calm mind.

41. A SOLUTION TO PROBLEMS IN WORLDLY LIFE.

"When a vehicle breaks down, not every driver knows how to repair it. But the manufacturer knows how to rectify any problems. Like this everyone living in the material world may not know how to face it when sorrows come in life. However, a Guru who is well versed in spiritual principles will know how to overcome sorrows from worldly life."

- Amma

Nowadays so many people drive different kinds of vehicles. However, if these vehicles break down along the way, how many know how to repair them? They must depend on the company that manufactured the vehicle or a repair shop.

This is exactly what happens in life also. Millions of people take refuge in Amma to get relief from the sorrows they experience in their worldly existence. Amma is a sage who has experienced True Knowledge, that which reveals all there is to know. In today's material world and life, we should recognize that there is no other Mahatma other than Amma who has given endless practical advice to all who approach her, regardless of caste or religion. In earlier times all the sages counseled those who came to them carrying the burden of worldly sufferings. There was a tradition of the Gurukula. Whoever attended were taught not just spiritual education, but also how to face life's challenges and sorrows without losing courage.

Those who had completed the Gurukula education then lived according to their Guru's instructions. Their life had an exalted goal. Their life was not fully drowned in materialism. Unfortunately, such a tradition of Gurukula no longer exists nowadays. The majority of people live weighed down by the burden of not knowing how to overcome the sorrows of worldly life and without understanding why they are experiencing them in the first place. Among such people, those who have earned merit in past lives, and those who are fortunate, reach a Guru who is Self-Realized and lead a contented life, realizing the goal of human life.

Let us take a look at what Amma says in this regard:

"Through family life what we have to do is to try and conquer our vasanas (our innate negative tendencies). "We should not drown in the vasanas. We should understand what they are and move forward. We will be able to reach our goal only if we achieve detachment from these vasanas, sooner or later. A person may eat sweet rice pudding to his stomach's fill and get up saying 'enough'. Yet after a while he will feel like eating twice the amount. If we realize how limited such pleasures are, then our mind will not run after them. No matter how much you may like sweet rice pudding, if a crow defecates in it, would you eat it?

"When the vasanas pull us towards them, we should remember that they are not the real source of joy, that they will be the cause of our sorrow tomorrow. Then the mind will not go there. This belief should be firmly established in our mind and intellect. Children, you should not be trapped by the thoughts in the mind and ruin your life by living like a slave. You should not sell a priceless diamond to purchase mere peanut candy. If we avoid the excessive importance we give to worldly affairs today, the mind will become much calmer. Children do not be sad thinking that you did not get the strength for this soon enough. Sit in solitude for some time daily, witness and reflect on your thoughts. Make this a habit. We will certainly be able to find the strength. It is no use crying, saying that we are weak. What is needed is to find and acquire the strength. This will help us transcend any situation without losing courage. It is useless to cry over the past. Once we are aware that only through knowing God can we get eternal peace, then such a discerning mind itself is a great achievement."

Amma narrates a story in this context:

"Once there lived a woodcutter, who was very poor. He would go into the forest daily, cut a tree into firewood, burn this wood, make charcoal, fill a sack, and take it to the charcoal store. However, his earnings from this were meager. It was not enough for even the bare minimum of food. His hut was leaky, old and rusted. Everyday he experienced nothing but unhappiness. His health was so poor that he couldn't work anymore.

"One day the king rode through this village. He heard about this poor man's plight and said, 'From now on you need not worry. I give you permission to cut all the trees from that forest you see. Ten generations can live happily on those earnings.' The next day also the woodcutter set out to cut wood. Since he now had his own forest, he did not have to wander in search of a tree to cut. As always, he cut one tree into firewood, burnt this wood into ash, and took it to his usual charcoal store. He did not earn any more money than before.

"Many days later when the king came that way again, he summoned the woodcutter. The king had assumed that he would have become a very wealthy man. But he was astonished when he saw the woodcutter. His condition was the same; actually, it was worse than before. There was not a trace of happiness on his face. Only disappointment. If you saw his face, you would think he had even forgotten to smile! The king asked with surprise, 'What happened to you? What did you do with the forest I gave you?' The woodcutter replied, 'I cut the wood and made charcoal and sold it.'

"The king was amazed to hear the woodcutter's reply. He had sold such valuable trees for such a paltry sum. He said, 'You fool! That was a sandalwood forest. Each tree was worth hundreds of thousands. Not to be burnt for charcoal and destroyed. Now how many trees are left?' The woodcutter replied, 'One.' The king said, 'At least there is one tree left. Instead of burning it for charcoal, cut it and sell the wood. You will earn enough to live from that.' The woodcutter, who followed the king's advice, got enough wealth from that one sandalwood tree to live happily for the rest of his life."

42. LIVE A WORRY-FREE LIFE

"If you drive after learning properly, then you can drive without tension. Similarly, if you live after learning the principles, you can live without tension."

- Amma

All of us must have, at one time or the other, travelled with someone who was not a good driver. Just think about how stressful that trip was! Wasn't it? Because the driver was flustered by unexpected obstacles, not knowing how to handle them, we suffered. However, someone who has learned driving well will be able to overcome these challenges effortlessly and move forward. Our lives too are like this. When we face obstacles in life, we become helpless. Some people even go as far as contemplating suicide.

Let us take a look at what Amma says about overcoming

debilitating situations in life.

"Spiritual science is that which helps us face the difficult situations in life. It is based on the experience of the Sages, and the teachings of the Mahatmas, who live out these teachings. That is why Amma says, not having this knowledge, the people today are like those sleeping under a tree with a cobra's nest in its branches. One who knows swimming enjoys even large waves. Those who cannot swim will get caught in them and suffer. Sometimes even death can occur.

"Spiritual epics like the Ramayana, Mahabharatha and the Bhagavatham have been composed for the ordinary person. Each of those stories contains a spiritual principle. When we study those and try to incorporate them in our lives, we will be able to find solutions to the problems in our lives.

"No man can live free of sorrows. Those who have not learned this science become helpless when faced with sorrows. Unable to overcome them, many lose their mental balance. Sometimes it even ends in suicide. However, one who has studied this science is aware of the nature of the world and worldly objects. Everything that is born must perish one day. Such is the case with our body, made up of the five elements, as well. When death nears, no one waits for anyone. Relationships are not permanent. Today's friend can become tomorrow's enemy. Today's enemy may be a friend tomorrow. When we understand this truth, the awareness rises in us that only God is Truth.

"This is why Amma says, 'The science of spirituality is the science of the mind. This is what we should learn first. If we attain victory over our mind, we attain victory over the world. It is this very same mind that is the cause of both bondage and liberation.'

"Manah Eva Manushyanam karanam bandhamokshayoh"! Right now, our mind is not in our hands, it is in the grip of our accumulated vasanas (negative tendencies). It is dangerous to live according to those.

"Once a man approached several Gurus. All of them would only speak about humility, awareness, and devotion. The man did not like this. He decided: 'I cannot be subordinate to anyone.' He left and sat on a roadside. He thought to himself, 'None of the Gurus I saw are capable of guiding me properly.' As he sat there thinking like this, he noticed a camel grazing the grass nearby bobbing its head. The man was amazed and thought, 'Oh! This camel understood what I was thinking in my mind! This is the Guru I have been searching for!' He approached the camel and asked, 'Would you be my Guru?' The camel again nodded its head. He was delighted.

"After this he would consult the camel Guru before he did anything. No matter what he asked the camel would nod his head and agree. One day he asked the camel, 'I have seen a girl. May I make her my girlfriend?' The camel nodded. A few days later he again came to the camel and asked, 'May I marry her?' The camel Guru was agreeable with this also. After some more time passed the man said, 'She is not giving me any peace of mind. Can I go drink?' The camel again nodded. So, the man went and drank to his heart's content and went home. Then it became a habit. The wife did not like this. Fights began in the house. He came to the camel Guru, 'Shall I fight with her?' he asked. The Guru agreed. Then it was nonstop arguments and fights with the wife. He visited the Guru again, 'I can no longer live with her. Shall I stab and kill her?' Then also the camel nodded. There was no delay after this. The man went home and stabbed his wife. Hearing this, the police arrived, arrested him, and put him in jail. He was sentenced to life imprisonment.

"Today our mind is like this camel Guru. Right or wrong is not an issue. We are completely agreeable to anything that the mind likes. There is no thought about consequences. If one obeys such a vasana-filled mind, the result will be permanent bondage. Right now, we do not have a discriminative mind. It is an emotional mind. Therefore, it is best if we live according to the Guru's instructions. When we do this, we can move forward in the journey of life without any tension, just as someone who has learned driving can drive without tension."

43. NOTHING IS INSIGNIFICANT

"A plane cannot fly if it loses even one screw. Even that screw has its own place and value. Likewise, nothing is insignificant in this universe. Everything has its own place and value."

- Amma

No matter how expensive a plane may be, how new the technology used to build it is, if it is missing even one screw, it will not be able to fly. As far as that large plane is concerned, that little screw is an indispensable component. If you think about it, a honeybee is such a small creature in this vast creation. Isn't it? And yet, it is only because this bee takes honey and pollen from each flower and deposits it on another flower that cross-pollination takes place. And because of this, we get flowers and fruits.

Once, after returning to Amritapuri after the Amritolsavam

celebrations at Kozhikode, Amma got down from the car. It was the time when the construction of the flats was going on in the Ashram. As Amma was walking through the front courtyard, her eyes fell upon tiny nails that were lying on the ground. Disregarding her tiredness after the long journey, Amma sat down there itself and began picking up the nails. Seeing this, those accompanying Amma, the Ashram residents and devotees, all began to pick up the broken, rusted, bent nails that were strewn around on the ground. Like this, within a short period of time, they were able to collect all the nails.

After this Amma said, "We should not see these nails as insignificant because so many people walk this way. Similarly, during Darshan days, countless visitors walk along this path. What will be their condition if they step on a nail, especially someone with diabetes? If it is a rusted nail, then the wound will become septic. Gangrene will develop where the nail went in. Wounds on diabetic people do not heal as quickly as in normal people. It is even possible that the toe may have to be amputated. Sometimes even the entire foot might have to be amputated. And if the infection does not go away the entire leg may have to be amputated. And in rare cases, the person could even die. If the person is the head of the family, then everyone who is dependent on him will suffer from this tragedy. See how a tiny nail can become the cause of grief in the lives of so many people! So, children, it is not right to disregard even an unusable nail thinking it insignificant.

"We should not consider any action in life as insignificant. Everything has its own value. In some situations, it could be with just a word, in others a smile, or doing something small to help. We may think that many things like this in our life are trivial. We have heard so many stories about seeing something big in something small, in our legends and history.

"During Amma's childhood the brooms were made with sticks from coconut spines. When sweeping the courtyard, Amma's biological mother, Damayanti Amma, would scold Amma if even a single bristle from the broom was lost. She would always say, 'Individual bristles together make a broom. So, do not see even one bristle as insignificant. Instead, in every bristle you should be able to see a broom.'

"We should not see one minute as insignificant. Because if we lose that one minute, we will never get it back. There have been so many instances when we have missed the bus, train etc. because we arrived one minute late! We should not see even a grain of rice as insignificant. We should remember the hardships of the people who worked to get that grain of rice in front of us."

In the above examples, the lessons that Amma shows us are not insignificant. Amma is constantly demonstrating to us with her own life that a loving smile, a compassionate glance, a kind word, a helping hand, all give hundreds of thousands of people peace and solace.

44. SEARCHING FOR THE MOST IMPORTANT THING

"Once a train stopped at a station. During this pause, a man got down to buy things. But he started haggling saying the price of what he bought was too much. In the end, after much argument, the seller reduced the cost by a small amount. By the time the man, happy with his victory returned, the train had already left. We are like this. It is because of arguing and fighting about petty things in life that we miss gaining the most valuable goal."

- Amma

This is very familiar to us. This is something that has surely happened to us or someone we know during a train journey. We stand arguing and bargaining for a small reduction in cost, and in the end, either the train leaves or we have to run and jump onto the moving train. We have also read about people who have fallen to their deaths while trying to jump aboard a moving train. What is the reason for this? It is the undue importance we give to unnecessary things.

Let us look at what Amma has to say about this: "Once there lived a rich man. One day his friends came to visit him. They asked the servant who was standing outside, 'Where is the master of the house?' The servant looked inside the house, returned, and told them, 'The master is counting stones.' The guests were astonished, 'Such a wealthy man, counting stones?' After some time when the man came out to meet them, they asked about this. The rich man was astonished, 'Is the servant such an idiot to think I was counting stones when I was counting money?' He said to his friends, 'Please forgive any inconvenience caused.'

"After the guests had left, the rich man called the servant and scolded him severely. A few days passed, and another friend came to see the master. He asked the servant to find his master. The servant checked inside the house and said, 'My master is busy loving his enemy.' That day also, the rich man was counting his money and locking it inside the cupboard. Thinking that the servant had deliberately insulted him, the rich man trembled with anger, 'Is he that arrogant?' He beat the servant and threw him out.

"As the servant was leaving, the master called out and gave him a doll saying, 'When you see anyone more idiotic than you, give him this doll!' The servant took the doll and walked away without saying anything. A few months passed by. One night when the rest of the family had gone out, robbers entered the rich man's house. They threatened the master and took all his money. When the master tried to resist, they pushed him off the top floor. The robbers escaped with all the cash.

"In the morning when the relatives returned, they saw the master lying in the front yard with a broken back. He could not stand up. Though various kinds of treatments were tried, nothing was helpful. In the end, he lost all of his wealth. With that, his children and wife abandoned him. The rich man lay there suffering in pain, without getting proper food or care. He ate if the neighbors gave him something. There was no one to pay him any attention.

"When the old servant heard about the master's troubles, he came to see him. The old doll was in the servant's hands. As soon as he saw him, he held out the doll to the rich man. The master understood. He asked, 'Are you rubbing salt in my wound?' The servant replied, 'I hope at least now you have understood the substance of what I said. With all the wealth that you had earned, are you getting the value of even a stone today? Wasn't it your wealth that became your enemy and reduced you to this state? Didn't you lose everything that you had from excessive wealth? Who could be a bigger idiot than you, who loved that kind of wealth? Those who loved you till now didn't love you. It was your money they loved. When the wealth was gone, you became just a dead body to them. Today everyone hates you. At least now, call out to God knowing that only He is your true friend.'

"We should understand the real nature of each and every object. We should become aware that material objects can never give us permanent happiness. Even though we may get temporary satisfaction by depending on these objects, it will end up bringing us sorrow. If we become fully aware of this truth, our attachment to them will reduce naturally. It will become easy to divert our mind from them.

"A man who loved rice pudding went to attend his friend birthday feast. Sure enough, the main dessert for the feast was rice pudding. He was overjoyed. He got a full bowl. He tasted one spoon. It was perfect, just enough sugar, milk, cardamom, raisins and cashews nuts! How delicious! As he took another spoonful, a lizard fell into the bowl of pudding from the ceiling. Both happened at the same time. Taking the entire bowl of his favorite pudding, he threw it out. The pudding was now not edible, he lost interest in it completely. Similarly, if we realize that pursuing objects of the worldly objects will only bring us sorrow, then we will be able to keep away from even those objects we love dearly. We won't have any difficulty in turning our mind away from that object or controlling our mind. This is called dispassion.

"When a child sees a cobra, it will try to catch it because he does not know it is poisonous. Would we do that? Until now, we had been thinking that the body is eternal. Understanding that it causes sorrow is a new experience for us. Now let us think this way: The Self is eternal. That is what we should realize. When this awareness becomes firm in us, we will discern the transient nature of sorrows. We have been wasting our time and this precious life in the pursuit of insignificant things. Like this, we depart from this world without having gained the goal of human life, Self-Realization. This is why Amma says that without recognizing the diamond within us, we waste our life on an insignificant handful of peanuts."

45. THE REAL PEACEMAKER

"A tanker truck caught fire. The driver called the fire force when he realized that he could not control the fire by himself. Though the fire force extinguished the fire, the truck was completely burned. But the tank had not caught fire. When opened the tank to check what it contained, it was fire extinguisher gas. This is how it is in our life as well. We depend on many things to find peace in life. Most times, it is when our life is ending without having found any peace that we find it within ourselves."

- Amma

During our travels we might have seen a tanker truck that had caught fire lying on the highway, completely destroyed, and sometimes the people in it may have died as well. However, what if the vehicle carrying fire extinguisher gas itself catches fire, and the same fire extinguishers must be brought from outside, to contain the fire? Similarly, we have bliss inside of us. This is like looking for bliss in alcohol and drugs without trying to find it within. We know, that nowadays countless people depend on alcohol for peace of mind. Finally, they wander around like stray dogs without being of any use to themselves, their family or to society and die a miserable death. The number of young people consuming drugs and wasting their lives living like lunatics is also increasing.

If we take a look at today's society, how many countless families are suffering difficulties due to alcohol abuse. So many thefts take place to get the money to buy alcohol. Today many are in prison, for murders committed when not in their senses while intoxicated. If we look at the root cause of all this, we will understand that they had all tried to find happiness outside of themsevles.

Let us see what Amma says on this topic -

"It is mere fallacy that intoxication gives happiness. Is bliss in beedis (hand-rolled cigarettes), cigarettes, alcohol, or marijuana? There are people who literally burn thousands of rupees every month on cigarettes. That money is enough to finance a child's education. These intoxicants may help to forget everything for a few moments. However, most times, what we were trying to forget will bounce back up with double the strength. Not just that, at that time, the person is damaged due to loss of vitality in the body, causing deteriorated health and untimely death. A person who is meant to be a benefactor for his family and society becomes a burden to himself, and harms others as well.

"It is because man seeks only selfish pleasures that he develops the habits of smoking and drinking. They think happiness lies in such things. We should teach such people spiritual principles. For this, firstly we ourselves should be ready to live according to these principles. Then others will see that and learn. Today most people have the attitude of me and mine. There is no thought outside of sensory pleasures for himself and his family. This selfishness is death. It destroys both the person as well as society. That is why Amma says that only through spiritual thinking can such a selfish mind be made expansive and understand that, 'Everything is one Atman. Everyone is the child of one mother, the Universal Mother. We all breathe the same air. I had no name, no caste when I was born. It is only many days after being born, that caste, religion etc. come into existence. So, forgetting those currently prevailing barriers, love everyone as children of the same mother. Help as necessary, that is my duty. It is only by loving and serving others that I can achieve true happiness in life. Helping the suffering is the true worship of God.' We should live with this attitude. Through this we will rise to expansiveness. When we imbibe these principles, our character will undergo a transformation. We will become compassionate towards others.

"Amma is not saying you should not have a wife, children, or family, instead of wasting life living like animals, learn to live with contentment. Live knowing the goal of life rather than just chasing after sensory pleasures. Lead a simple life. Take what you need and give the rest to charity. Live without harming anyone. Teach this to others also. We have to give this kind of good culture to the world. Create a good mind for yourself. Through that, make others good also. This is what we need. When that happens, even if the external comforts lessen, we will always feel increasing peace and contentment inside.

"We will never be able to find perfection in the outside world.

Even so, in today's world, man is constantly searching for perfection and happiness in the external world. Many women come and tell Amma, 'Amma I am 40 years old. But am still unmarried'. Similarly, men also come and tell Amma, "Amma at this age, I am still unmarried. I am still searching for the wife of my dreams. I have not found her yet.' Like this, both are disappointed, and life becomes filled with sorrow.

"Two friends met each other at a hotel after a very long time. The first man said, 'Oh, I am glad I met you, because my marriage has been fixed. You should come'. 'Sure, I can come', agreed the friend. 'Okay, so, your marriage has not happened yet. What is the reason? Is it because you decided against marriage?' 'No, I am interested in getting married. But I was searching for the all-perfect woman. I met a woman in Spain. She was both beautiful and intelligent. She was also interested in spirituality. However, she knew nothing about life in the world. So, I decided against that. Later in Korea I met another young lady. She was not only beautiful and intelligent, but also well versed in the ways of the world. But she talked too much! And like that, my search continued. Finally in another country I met the wife of my dreams. She was faultless. Perfect in all ways! We had no difficulty in getting along.' 'So then, did you marry her?', the friend asked eagerly. 'No', the man replied dejectedly. 'Why, what happened?' 'Oh, well, she too was searching for the perfect man.'

"This is why Amma says, 'Children if you search for perfection on the outside, you will always be disappointed.' What are all human beings searching for? Isn't it peace and happiness? Man is running around for a bit of peace. Yet peace and contentment have disappeared from our midst. We are striving hard to make the external world into a heaven. But we are unaware that our inner world has become like hell. There is no dearth of objects for comfort and pleasure in today's world. There is no peace of mind even after living in air-conditioned rooms. There are those who sleep in these kinds of rooms and take sleeping pills, not being able to sleep. Many living amid luxury commit suicide unable to handle their mental conflicts.

"If happiness and contentment were in material objects, they should have received that from a life of luxury. However, this is not what we see. If only those who rush to air-condition their homes and cars would learn to 'air-condition' their minds first! That is the only path to true happiness. Spirituality is the science that teaches us how to air-condition the mind. It is training of the mind. That is true learning."

Peace, contentment and happiness are all dependent on our mind. Not on external objects or situations. Victory over the mind, that is the foundation of happiness. Heaven and hell - both are the creations of the mind. If the mind is peaceful, the worst hell can become heaven. If the mind is agitated even the highest heaven will seem like hell. Spiritual science is a science that teaches us how to build a life filled with peace and happiness in the middle of worldly contradictions.

46. IT IS DEFERENCE...

"We put oil and grease in our vehicle from time to time. Otherwise, the vehicle's noises and whining will be loud. Likewise, it is deference that brings discipline to society. If it is not there, noise and commotion will keep happening in life."

- Amma

Amma is saying that a sense of deference is essential in life. That is what brings about harmony in society. Only when we respect those who have knowledge, age, position, and experience will there be orderliness in society. Many a time, lack of deference causes conflicts.

For normal vehicles, we need to grease and oil the engine from time to time. Otherwise, it will become noisy. The drivers who know this will grease and oil the vehicle even before the noises are noticeable.

We can see that many of the challenges in today's homes are due to lack of deference. The younger family members do not want to accept the knowledge and wealth of experience of the elders, which gives rise to various problems. Like this there are so many families in our society that have lost the ability to live harmoniously. This is among the most important values lost to the new generation.

Amma says: "In the old days, men would unfold the Mundu (dhoti) to its full length to cover their legs when they saw elders in the community. If they had a cloth tied around their heads, they would remove that also and hold it in their hands. However today, we see the father and the son sitting together and sharing the same bottle of alcohol. We see them smoking a beedi or cigarette from the same packet. Their response to all this is that the old customs are outdated and that the new way is more practical.

This reminds me of an incident from my school days. In my school there were about 2700 students studying from the first to the tenth standard. The teacher who taught the fourth standard was very strict. If any student from the first to the tenth standard uttered any kind of curse word, someone or the other would go and report it to this teacher. Immediately the student would be summoned. The teacher would take a slate (used for writing) from a student. He would write on it in large letters, "From now on I will never utter a curse word." Then he would call the student who cursed, place the slate in his hands and tell him, "Place this on your head in such a way that everyone can read it. Then you should go to each of the 70 classrooms and stand in front of the students for 10 seconds. After that come back and return the slate to me."

The student would do as instructed. Never again in his life would he use a curse word! This teacher did this throughout his tenure at the school. No parent ever came with a complaint, neither did any student try to commit suicide because of this punishment. And when the students left this school after ten years of studies, their most affectionate farewell would be to this teacher. Even today, everyone remembers that as a sweet memory.

However, what is today's condition? If any teacher tried to do this, the child will first try to commit suicide. Will the parents let this go? Next, the human rights commission, the child rights commission, the parent teacher association, and social media would all rail against this teacher. This is the kind of attitude that destroys the discipline and orderliness of life, whether in the family or in society.

That is the reason Amma says, "Through obeying and respecting our parents, teachers, and elders, we ourselves were growing, gaining knowledge, and cultivating good values and behaviors. Humility will only bring progress. The seed has the tree in it. However, if the seed stays in the granary proudly claiming this fact, it will end up becoming food for the rats! It is only when it bows its head to the soil and goes under it that its true nature is revealed. When you press the button on an umbrella, it opens. It is then able to save others from the rain and sun. Who wants an umbrella that does not open?

"I am asking you all to show humility to others so that we can awaken the good tendencies that are within us. Humility is not a weakness. Whenever we show anger and behave arrogantly with others with the attitude that 'I am an important person', we are losing the power within us at that time. We are losing sight of the divinity within us. Nobody wants to be the humble one. The reason we lack humility is because of our pride in illusory things. This body of ours is a form filled with ego, the sense of 'I'. Our mind is polluted with arrogance, desire, and anger. It is to purify such a mind that I am asking you to cultivate humility and modesty. When we behave arrogantly, body-consciousness is increasing. In order to destroy this arrogance, we should have the willingness to prostrate to our Gurus and behave humbly towards them.

"If we pour clean water into a dirty bucket, the water will only get spoiled. If we mix tamarind with sweet pudding and eat it, we will not know the taste of the pudding. Similarly, if we remain arrogant when we do our spiritual practices, we will not be able to surrender completely to God, understand the results of our spiritual practices, or experience the benefits. When we reduce our arrogance through humility and modesty, our good qualities emerge, we are expanding the Jivatma (the individual soul) within us to the Paramatman (the Supreme Soul).

"Today we are like a table lamp. It can only give enough light to read the book in front of it. But the room light illuminates an entire room. What to say of the sun? If we understand this one weakness of ours, we will be able to bring deference, and obedience into our lives. Otherwise, there will be recurring noisy discord in life."

47. NEED WE FEAR?

"We control our speed while driving, because of the traffic cameras on the road. And not out of a sense of duty. Similarly, it is fear of punishment by God that generally prevent people from wrongdoing. Not love for God."

- Amma

While traveling we often see the speeding vehicle in front of us slowing down suddenly. And when we look, we see that there is a camera in that spot. He did not reduce his speed because he was aware that driving fast could cause danger to him and others. This camera will record the speed of the vehicle, and he will have to pay the fine. He slowed down because of this fear.

Just like this, many of us refrain from wrongdoing only because we believe that God will punish us if we do so, not because of a sense of righteousness. In homes where the children do not misbehave, it is because they are afraid of their parents. Children in the lower grades study because they are afraid their teachers will punish them. It is not because of the awareness that it is their duty to study. Similarly, when we interact with society, we do not commit wrongs because we are afraid of the police and the courts. Even here, our correct behavior is not due to awareness of moral conduct or honesty.

Let us see what Amma has to say.

"Ninety-nine percent of religious people visit places of worship to escape from life's difficulties, not out of love for God. There are those who go to places of worship out of fear of God's punishment in case they do something wrong, or to atone for any wrongs they have already committed. And some also go to places of worship to stop committing sins, or for fulfilment of desires. I do not say that any of these are wrong. All of it is good. Yet, life should not stop at just this.

"Doesn't Amma say, you may take birth in a temple, but do not die there! What is the meaning of this? It is alright if devotion begins with temple visits, but we should not be confined to that till the end of our lives. It should proceed from this stage to visiting spiritual Gurus and understanding some scriptural sciences as well. We should take refuge in a Self-Realized master and try to learn from their life. Then we will realize that true devotion is love for God. It is when our hearts melt in that love for God that our worldly sorrows become non-existent. Right now, our mind is in the objects of the world. It is not possible to forcefully remove it from them. However, it is very easy for us to attach the mind to something that is much dearer to us than these. Our effort should be towards developing this longing for God, that intense love inside us.

Because of our ignorance, we are unable to experience God. It is through Mahatmas that we are able to experience the presence of God. It is like this - we cannot see electricity with our eyes. Yet touch your finger to a wire through which electric current is running! Then you will experience it. The God principle is also not a belief but an experience. We have to know the Divine through personal experience.

"When we stand in the shade of a tree, we do not see the shining sun in the sky. You could say that the tree is hiding the sun. Not true. The tree is not big enough to hide the sun. The tree is just hiding the sun from our sight. In the same way, due to ignorance, we are unable to see God.

"Dharma is the life secret that teaches one to love and serve, forgive, and tolerate one another and treat each other with kindness. Advaita, the foundation of Santana Dharma, is each person's individual experience. Still, it can be manifested in daily life in the form of love and compassion. It is this great lesson that the Gurus and the sages of Santana Dharma are teaching us.

"The language of religion that we have forgotten is the language of compassion. We have forgotten the language of love and mutual trust that religions teach us. The root cause of all the problems we see in the world today is the lack of love and compassion. The cause of problems in the life of individuals, nations and even the world at large, is that we cannot assimilate the teachings of love and compassion advised by religions. Like food and sleep, spirituality should become an indispensable part of our life. We need to give Religion new life and vigor. Only then will love and compassion grow in our hearts. Only love and compassion can remove the darkness and spread light and purity throughout the world.

"Love is everywhere. However, not every form of love we see in the world is true love. We love our family members but do not love our neighbors the same way. We are not prepared to love other children the same way we love our own son or daughter. We do not love others the same way we love our own father and mother. So, ours is not true love. It is an attachment with limitations. The goal of spirituality is to transform this narrow, limited attachment into divine love."

This is the reason Amma says that true devotion is the ability to see others as ourselves. There is no sense of separateness, and in that state, there is no place for wrong doing. Then we will become aware that God is not someone who punishes us, but someone who protects us. This is the devotion and love that we should attain.

48. FIRST SELF-EFFORT, THEN GOD'S WILL

"Before going on a long journey, we should check our vehicle's oil level, water level and tire pressure. This is the effort needed from our side. The rest should be left to God's will. Similarly, on the journey of life, we should do our duty. The rest should be left to God's will."

- Amma

If we pay attention to a cab driver, we will notice that before he takes his car out for the day, he will check the oil and water levels, the air pressure in the tires, the spare tire, the carjack, etc. Only after he is sure these are all fine will he start driving. By doing this, accidents are prevented. These are all efforts from our part. Even then we may still meet with an accident. How? If the driver coming from the opposite direction is asleep at the wheel, drunk or driving carelessly, it can also affect us. That is not in our hands. We should consider this to be God's will. This is the only way we can move forward without losing our peace of mind. If a child writes an exam without studying and fails, it is pointless to blame God. Because he went for the exam without fulfilling his duty. How will God be able to help him?

Similarly, while living in society, parents, children, government officials, the citizenry, doctors, engineers, all of them have their own dharma (individual duty). Parents love, educate and guide their children onto the right path. These are the efforts from their part. If the children go on the wrong path, there is no use blaming God. Only if the parents teach the children about dharma (right moral conduct) and lead a righteous life themselves will the children live according to that.

According to Indian tradition after a couple gets married, has one or two children, educates them and gets them married, then they should lead a Vanaprastha life (partial retirement from worldly life). They hand over the rest of the family responsibilitics to the children. It is because the parents are not living by the true values that the children fail to behave in a correct manner with them. It is such children who leave their aging parents in old age homes. But we cannot blame the children alone. It is because the parents never taught the children ethical principles. How can we expect the children to live and behave according to values they were never taught?

Let us also look at what Amma says...

"We must have the awareness that remembrance of God is most important. If we have this awareness, then we will be able to find time for everything. If we don't have this then we will make excuses for not doing Sadhana, saying that we have no time. The mind is always like this. When it is time to do auspicious things, it will find many reasons not to do it.

"Once a businessman approached his Guru and said 'Guru, I have no peace of mind. It is very difficult. What should I do?' The Guru said 'I will give you a mantra. It is enough to chant it continuously.' 'Guru, how will I, who am busy throughout the day with many different responsibilities, find the time to chant?' Hearing the wealthy man's reply the Guru asked, 'Where do you go for your bath?' 'In the river nearby', said the man. 'How much time does it take you to get there?' 'Three minutes,' the man replied. The Guru said, 'Then do one thing, you can chant from the time you leave your house until you reach the river. Try doing this.'

"After a few months the man came to the Guru with great enthusiasm. After prostrating he said, 'All my mental turmoil has vanished. My mind is peaceful. I am chanting the mantra you gave me without fail. Now, I cannot keep myself from chanting the mantra. At first, I chanted when I was going for my bath. Then I made it a habit to chant while bathing and while returning home. Then I began chanting while going to work. Later if I remembered about the mantra while working, I would start chanting. I started chanting while going to bed. I fall asleep chanting the mantra. Because of this, as soon as I wake up, the mantra resumes. The chanting in the mind goes on during the daily activities. As the days pass by, I feel the desire to increase my chanting. Now it is difficult for me not to chant.' Due to constant effort, chanting became a habit, even for this extremely busy man.

"It is not enough to just say that it is difficult. We must also think about how much effort we have made towards it. It is because we lack proper understanding and are not doing what is required at the right time that our sorrows are not ending.

"If we water the roots of a tree, all the top branches and the leaves will also get it. On the other hand, there is no benefit in watering just the top. Similarly, no one benefits from just worrying about things. However, if we offer our mind to God, if we take refuge in him, then we will not want for anything. We will get everything we need. Problems will get resolved somehow. There will be peace and contentment in life. It is God's resolve that those who sincerely meditate and pray to Him will never lack necessities. This is also Amma's experience. If nothing else, it is enough to chant the Sri Lalitha Saharanamam with love and devotion regularly. If you do this, you will not lack at least food and clothes. No matter what you may possess, without doing Sadhana it is not possible to have peace of mind. No matter how much wealth you may have, if you want to sleep with ease at night, you should take refuge in God. Do not forget to remember God, even if you forget to eat.

"Before we fall asleep every night, we should sincerely examine ourselves. 'Today at how many people did I get angry? How much time was I able to devote to prayer? How much time did I waste in selfish actions? How much money did I spend on luxuries?' Such a self-evaluation should become a part of our daily sadhana."

Complete surrender is the essence of Amma's teachings. No matter what our problems may be, if we place it in God's hands and move forward, we will not become exhausted by them. It is in the light of her own life experiences that Amma is assuring us that God will take care of all our matters.

49. CONSTANT REPETITION PROTECTS

"Children after you get on the bus do not be careless because you have bought a ticket. Keep the ticket safe. If you don't show it when asked, you will be let down from the bus. Similarly, do not consider all is done, just because you have received a mantra. Only if you use it the way it should be used will it get you to where you need to reach."

- Amma

Let us take a look at what Amma says about the importance of chanting a mantra.

"We know that when we travel by train or bus, the ticket examiner comes and checks our tickets. We are obliged to show him our ticket. Otherwise, they have the authority to kick us off the train or make us pay the fare right from where the vehicle started. Just like this, when we take a mantra from the Guru, it is our duty to keep it safely in the pocket of our mind. Why would God need a mantra? The mantra is to cleanse our minds and is not to be used as a tool to please God. It is enough if we chant the mantra. There is no need to worry yourself sick about its meaning. When we travel to the Ashram we come by bus, car or train. We do not waste time thinking about the mechanical workings of that vehicle. We just need to be aware of the destination. Whichever mantra the Guru gives us, it will be able to get us there. We chant the mantra to remove mental impurities and develop concentration.

"When the weeds that are mental impurities are removed, the substratum of the mind can be seen with clarity, making it easier for meditation as well. We should never habituate the mind to chant the mantra carelessly, without attention. We should avoid other thoughts as much as possible when we chant. We should take care to focus our mind on a form or the syllables of the mantra.

"We should train the mind to chant continuously without rest. When it is like that, the mind will continue to chant when we perform any action. A spider is always spinning a web wherever they are. Like this the mantra should always continue in our mind no matter what we may be doing.

"During meditation if we lose the form of the deity, we should again imagine the form, visualize binding our beloved deity from the feet to the head with the rope of mantra, and again untying him. This will help keep our mind tied to the form of the beloved deity.

"The mind is like a cat. No matter how much food we may give the cat, or pamper it, if our attention is diverted even for a second, it will steal food. In order to tame such a mind, and make it focused, one should constantly chant the mantra. While walking, sitting, or working, the mantra should continue to flow like a stream of oil. In the old days, if Amma took one step without chanting her mantra, she would take two steps backwards, then move forward only after chanting the mantra.

"Each and every mantra in the Sahasranamam has extremely deep meanings. The very first mantra itself is 'Aum Sri Matre Namah'. The meaning is 'Salutations to She who is the Mother'. A mother is the embodiment of patience. When we chant this mantra, that attitude of a mother will awaken in us. Like that, the mantra is helping to develop patience in us as well. Each mantra in the Sahasranamam has as much significance as a mantra in the Upanishads. By chanting these mantras, we are unknowingly rising up to expansiveness. Currently our mind has the nature of a fly, flitting from excreta to honey, one after the other. Chanting the Sahasranamam elevates our mind from that level to Divine Consciousness. This is true Satsang!

"Once there were two children. The father would always take one child along with him wherever he went. Even when the father played cards with his friends, the child would sit nearby. When he drank alcohol, the child would also be with him. The mother kept the second child with her. She narrated inspiring stories to this child. Whenever she went to the temple, she would take this child along. Finally, the child who grew up with the father became an alcoholic and a gambler. There were no bad qualities that he did not possess.

"The child who grew up with the mother only spoke of good things, sang only devotional songs. He developed the attitude of love, compassion and humility in his interactions with others.

Like this, any circumstance can influence our tendencies. By chanting the Sahasranamam, and temple worship, we are awakening the divine qualities in us. Japa and mediation done with concentration can awaken the power within us. Additionally, those vibrations are beneficial for the environment as well.

"If we have a one-pointed resolve, anything is possible. However, people nowadays are unable to believe such things. Many years ago, when it was known that the satellite Skylab was going to fall to Earth, scientists asked everyone to mentally visualize it falling into the ocean. They were acknowledging that concentrated collective visualization has a lot of power. Everyone believed it when the scientists said it. The power of the mind and of mantra chanting was understood by the Sages so many ages ago. It is difficult for us to believe that. What scientists claim today, they themselves end up correcting tomorrow. Yet, if they say anything, we are ever willing to believe them.

"Through mantra japa an effort is being made to awaken the divinity within us. When we sprout beans, its vitamins and nutrients are increased. Similarly, Japa is a process which helps awaken the latent energy within us. Not only this, but Nature is also purified through the vibrations of the chanting. We will realize where the mind is when we close our eyes. Even if we are physically in the Ashram, the mind is on the things to do after reaching home. Which bus will be available for the return trip? Will it be crowded? We will see hundreds of thoughts like these running around in our mind. To transform such a mind, covered with hundreds of thoughts, into one focused on the Divine form is not something that can be achieved in a moment. Constant effort is required. Mantra Japa is an easy way towards this.

"If we run to catch a small child, he will run. If we too run behind him, he may fall into a pond or nearby well. Yet if we show him a toy, he will turn and come towards us. We can avoid the risk of him falling. Like this, mantra japa is the best method to bring the mind to an orderly state based on its true nature. If a hundred thoughts arise in the mind in a second, by chanting a mantra, these thoughts can be reduced to ten.

"We may ask, are there no thoughts in the mind when we chant a mantra. Even if thoughts arise, it is not so important. A thought is like a small child. When the child is asleep it is not difficult for the mother to attend to her work. Similarly, the thought that arises when we are chanting the mantra is of no consequence. It will not bother us.

"Some may ask, isn't the mantra itself a thought? Doesn't the one-line sign, 'Stick no bills' on a wall help prevent the wall from being covered with many advertisements? Similarly, with the one thought of the mantra it is possible to stop the wandering of the mind. The lesser the number of thoughts, the better it is for a person's lifespan and health. The warranty period of an object in the store is calculated only from the time we purchase it. There is no problem if it sits in the store for however many years because it is not operational. Likewise, when there are no thoughts, the strength of the mind does not decrease, it only increases. Our health improves, and we live longer. On the contrary, when thoughts increase, mental strength decreases. The health of the body is destroyed.

"We know stories of people from ages past, who did intense penance by standing on one leg, or lying on a bed of nails, to bring the mind under control. Nowadays we don't have to do anything like that. Mantra chanting is sufficient. The others realized God only after scriptural study and penance through many eras. Yet, the Gopis of Vrindavan did not learn scriptures. They were householders who lived with their family and children. They were milkmaids. Yet, through their intense love for Bhagavan, through constant remembrance, they were able to realize him quickly. Like that, especially in this Kali Yuga, devotion filled mantra japa is important.

"However, simply doing Japa and Sadhana is not the whole story. Only when one completely surrenders the mind to the Divine can one attain him. But how do we surrender the mind? It is not possible to pick it up and offer it. One surrenders the mind only by surrendering everything that it is attached to. Today the mind is most attached to wealth. After getting married, the mind dwells more on wealth, than on the wife or children. Even when the mother is dying, when the property is being partitioned, the thought is to try and get that land with the additional 10 coconut trees. If he gets slightly lesser than his sibling, some children will not even hesitate to kill the father. So where is our attachment? It is to wealth!

When we surrender the objects that our mind is attached to, we can say the mind has been surrendered. When those with minds attached to wealth use it for serving others, this too is surrender of the mind. Through this the mind is becoming expansive, becoming a vessel to receive God's grace. God has no need for all this wealth. These are the important aspects of mantra chanting."

50. WHEN TIME AND PLACE CHANGE...

"Even though the driving laws are the same within a country, they do not work the same everywhere. Vehicles do not drive on country roads the same way they do on express highways. Similarly, though dharma (moral conduct) is the same for everyone, the way it is used can differ based on time, country, and situation."

– Amma

We all know that in one country there is only one set of driving laws. These rules vary though, depending upon the condition of the road. We cannot drive on a highway at the same speed as on an express highway. Also, we cannot drive on village roads, or regional roads like we do on a highway. All vehicles are not permitted to drive on all roads. On some roads, only small vehicles like a bicycle are allowed. Some roads are meant for large container trucks. Freight carriers are not allowed on some roads during the daytime. So, the rules are enforced differently based upon the time, place, and situation.

This is what we see in life also. For example, until recently, parents in India had the authority to spank and scold their children. In some other countries spanking a child is illegal. This shows the differences from one country to the other.

Changes with reference to time are also similar. In earlier times, if children came to school without studying, or did something wrong, they would be scolded, caning was also prevalent. Nowadays, will the student allow the teacher to punish him like this? Will the parents agree to this? Moreover, will the human rights commission allow this? They will take legal action against such behavior. This is an example of changes according to time.

Let us see how Amma shows us that everyone may not be able to follow dharma at all times.

"That is why Amma says that for peace and contentment to prevail in society, awareness of dharma (right conduct) is essential. It is when selfishness and arrogance increase among people that righteousness and justice diminish in society. It may be possible for the police and the courts to apprehend and punish those who commit crimes with the help of modern scientific methods. Yet, this alone is not enough to awaken morality in people. This is possible only through spirituality. Spirituality is the science that teaches us to see others as ourselves. Man becomes selfish and arrogant because he does not have the right knowledge about the nature of the world and God's power.

"A person may be selfish, cruel, and arrogant today. Still even such a person has divinity in him. Even if a person has committed a hundred murders, doesn't his heart fill with love and affection when he sees his own child? Like embers covered by ash, goodness and love are definitely hidden within him as well. When we accept a person with love, forgetting his mistakes and faults, the essence of love within him will awaken. He will transform into a good human being. Only pure love has the power to bring about transformation in another human being.

"This is what the story of Maharishi Valmiki teaches us. When the Saptarishis (the Seven Sages) compassionately accepted Ratnakaran, who was then living by robbing and killing, he became Maharishi Valmiki. He realized that a selfish life was meaningless. He became an example for the whole world. Later, seeing a hunter shoot and kill a bird, he cried out with a stricken heart, 'No! Hunter', beseeching the hunter to stop. He was able to experience the pain of the bird as his own pain. The love of the seven sages was able to transform a cruel mind into a compassionate one.

"Once a daughter from France came to the Ashram. She was someone who loved luxuries. She only wore expensive clothes. When a new style of clothes, shoes, or handbags were released in the stores, she would buy them immediately. After she returned to France from the Ashram, she wrote Amma a letter. She said, 'Amma I had never experienced even a moment's peace in my life until I met you. Whenever I would see someone wearing nice clothes, I would be upset that the dress I was wearing was not as expensive. Then I would want a nicer dress than that. I would buy it even if I had to borrow the money. One day I went to a store to buy an expensive watch. There were watches ranging from 100000 euro studded with precious gems to those that were 10 euro. I thought to myself, I only need to know the time.

Even a watch costing 10 euro is sufficient for that. I can help so many poor people with the money that I have saved to purchase an expensive watch.

"The images of the beggars, orphaned children and sick people suffering in pain that I had seen during my travels appeared in my mind. I remembered their faces, helpless cries, and their pain. I did not think further. I bought the 10 euro watch and left the shop. I felt an unknown happiness and contentment in my mind. That night I slept peacefully. After that, I would not feel envious even if I saw someone wearing an expensive outfit. When I remember that I am able to help bring some relief to those suffering, my mind would fill with happiness.

"Children, for this daughter, the pain of others became her own. When her heart melted at their sorrow, the mind was filled with compassion. Selfishness and arrogance disappeared. A sense of morality awakened in her. We are not isolated islands but are connected like links in a chain. When we realize this, our life will have the right values. A person who lives according to values will never be able to hurt someone by thought, word or deed. On the contrary, they will become a source of support and solace to all. This is the practical side of spirituality. Only when we understand this, will we know how and where to practice our dharma.

51. WHEN WE DRIVE A BOAT ON LAND

"However nice a boat is, it cannot be driven on dry land. It is like this when we strive to find happiness in the external world."

- Amma

We all know no matter how large a boat may be, how well equipped it may be, or how many people it can accommodate, we cannot drive it on the road. Why? It has not been built for that purpose. Similarly, Amma says that bliss is within us, we should not be searching for it among external objects. We will never find it there.

Amma illustrates this truth further with an example:

"In reality, we are the embodiments of bliss. Without knowing this we depend on external objects for happiness. External objects of the world will never be able to give us perfect or permanent happiness. If happiness were in these objects, then the more we use them, the more happiness we would get. However, is this the case? Let's say we love rice pudding. If happiness were in the pudding, our happiness would increase with every bowl, but is that how it is? The happiness we get from eating the first bowl of pudding is not the same as after eating the second bowl. If we eat three, four or five bowls, and continue, after a while we will start hating it. Isn't it so? If happiness is in an object, the more we consume it, the more our happiness should increase."

"When a dog is relishing chewing a bone, he is actually enjoying the blood from the cuts on his own gums. The dog does not know this. He thinks that the blood is oozing from the bone. It is due to ignorance of this one truth that we humans also accumulate outside objects for our happiness."

"In today's world we see people purchasing and accumulating acres of land. If you ask them whether they have achieved complete contentment, the answer would be 'no'. We can ask millionaires, 'Are you happy'. Their reply would also be 'No'. If you ask those who have earned and amassed many external objects if they are perfectly happy with those things, the answer would be, 'No.' If Siddhartha, who was a prince, was fully happy, why did he leave the palace and his family and embark on a journey seeking relief from all suffering?

"Through family life, we should try to overcome our vasanas (latent tendencies) not simply drown in them. We should move forward understanding the nature of these tendencies. Today or tomorrow, we must develop dispassion towards these desires, only then can we reach the goal. Even if we get up saying 'enough' after eating our favorite food to our fill, after some time we will want to eat it even more. Still, if we realize it is like this, then the mind will not run after them. No matter how much we love a particular food, if even a drop of kerosene falls into it, will we eat it?

"Once we understand that vasanas will be the cause of sorrow tomorrow, our mind will not go towards them when they pull at us. They are not the true source of happiness. However, this realization should become firm in our mind and intellect. We must not destroy our life, living like slaves, enslaved by the desires of the mind. This is like selling a priceless gem to buy peanut candy. If we can stop giving material objects the excessive importance that we do now, the mind will calm down to a large extent.

"This is the reason Amma says that spirituality is the knowledge and realization that the source of happiness is within us only. Today we believe that happiness lies in objects. If that were the case, would not owning these objects make us completely satisfied? However, we see billionaires who own yachts, and private jets, living with stress and unhappiness. When one person enjoys smoking his cigarette, another starts coughing, and moves away covering his nose, unable to stand the smoke. Does this not prove that joy is not in the object. Happiness depends on our mind. Spirituality is the means to bring the remote control of that mind into our own hands.

"In a village two families lived in huts right next to each other. One of these men went abroad and earned a lot of money and built a large house. The neighbor became very sad, 'He now has a large house, but I am still living in this hut.' Thinking like this, the man got upset. With that, he started working without taking any rest and earned a little money. He borrowed the remaining amount and started building a house. The man spent each day, dreaming of living happily in his new house. When the construction was completed, the man felt such joy! He threw a feast for his friends and relatives and started living happily in the new house. A few months passed by. One day a friend saw him looking despondent and asked, 'Why are you sad again?' The man replied, 'My neighbor's house now has two stories. He has finished the floors in marble. It's a first-class, air-conditioned house! Look at my house what good is it?'

"The very same house that had until recently brought him joy, now caused him unbearable sorrow. From this we can understand that joy and sorrow are not dependent on external objects but on our state of mind. Therefore, we need to bring the mind under our control. Even if the house is air-conditioned and has all the modern amenities, if the husband and wife are not compatible, such a house will be like hell. They won't be able to sleep for even one night without taking sleeping pills. There are many people in such homes who commit suicide. In truth, it is the mind that should be air-conditioned. That is what spirituality teaches. Mahatamas are those who teach us this. When we take refuge in them, the tendency of the mind to run outwards stops. Then we understand that real happiness is within.

52. A SAFE DISTANCE

"While learning to drive when one first takes the vehicle on the road, one should maintain extra distance from the vehicle ahead. Like this, when starting spiritual practices, the spiritual aspirant should keep a distance from the opposite sex."

- Amma

Amma is talking about the things a spiritual seeker should pay attention to in the beginning. Let us take a look.

"When someone who is learning driving takes the vehicle on the road initially, they should always maintain a safe distance from the vehicle in front of him. Why? The vehicle in front could apply its brakes at any minute. Since he does not have much experience with driving, it is possible for him to crash into the vehicle in front of him. So, one should always maintain a good distance.

Similarly, in the beginning a spiritual seeker should always maintain distance from all kinds of sense objects.

"When we first plant a sapling, we should build a fence around it to protect it. Otherwise, a goat or cow will come and eat it up. When this sapling grows and becomes a big tree, there is no problem even tying an elephant to it. A spiritual seeker is also like this. During the initial stages of spiritual practice, he should stay away from worldly people. Later, once he has gained the power to guide people, he will be able to give them appropriate advice. Though we have awareness of the goal, it has not become fully established. That is why I am saying that we should keep away from unfavorable circumstances. We have heard so many stories in the puranas (old legends) of seekers who got trapped like this.

"Once, in an Ashram the Guru gave Sannyasa diksha (monastic initiation) to his senior disciples. Only one disciple in that group did not receive Sannyas. The man became very angry with the Guru. He started criticizing the Guru to others. The Guru happened to hear about this. Then, pretending not to know anything, the Guru called the disciple and said, 'From today on you should go daily to the village nearby and purchase milk for everyone.' So, the disciple started going there every day to buy milk. There was a beautiful young woman who used to measure the milk and distribute it.

"After a few days the disciple came and told the Guru. 'Guru, I would like to tell you something.' The Guru asked him to speak. 'My mind is always remembering the young woman in the village where I go to buy milk. I am unable to forget her. So, I have decided to marry her.' Hearing this the Guru said, 'Okay if that is your wish, please go ahead. However, now do you understand why I did not give you Sannyas. Though you have awareness of the goal, it was not strongly established. You do not yet have the ability to transcend situations.'

"It is true that in the old days people would go to the Himalayas to meditate. However, they did that only after they had finished leading a selfless householder life, attaining mental maturity and purity, and after relinquishing all their wealth. The surroundings in those days were also conducive to performing spiritual austerities. In comparison, the people then had assimilated spiritual principles more. Government officials were honest. Householders lived with the goal of God-realization. But people are more selfish these days. Today there are only family members, no Grihastashramis (householders observing ethical principles). They do not even know what selfless service is. So, these days, it is the spiritual people who do spiritual practices and penance. It is they who must show the world the model for selfless service.

"The disciple should not imitate all the actions of the Guru. This will create obstacles in his growth. It is not possible for anyone to fully imitate the Guru anyway. We should use our discrimination and adopt those actions which will be beneficial to us. We should try to copy only those from the Guru. We should never think, 'The Guru did such and such, so why can't I do that as well?' The Mahatmas who have attained completeness do not have constraints. Mahatmas enriched with penance are like the big trees strong enough to tie even an elephant. Trees do not need a fence. We on the other hand are like little saplings. We should fear the goats and cows. We need a fence so that they do not destroy us. However, once the same sapling has grown into a tree, we can tie the goat and cow to it. The world of the Mahatmas and their actions are not like ours. We should not imitate all their actions.

"An ordinary person's actions originate from body consciousness. They only have the awareness of 'I am the body'. The Mahatmas however live in the awareness that they are 'pure consciousness'. As such, ordinary people find it difficult to understand many of their actions.

"Once there was a Mahatma. Every morning he would pour boiling oil on his body after waking up. Only after this would he go for his bath. Seeing this one of the disciples thought that this boiling oil was the reason for all his Guru's powers and abilities. The next morning, the disciple also boiled oil and poured it over his body. What was the result? This could happen to us also, if we try to exactly emulate every action of the Guru. Therefore, we should only accept what is beneficial for each one of us.

"As long as materialistic thoughts agitate us, to rise above them, we should regularly do meditation and mantra practices with discipline. We should practice this properly for a long time. Then it will develop into a natural habit. Only spiritual practices will bring results. Those with no spiritual routine are people with nothing. What is the use of reading a lot and giving talks? What is the difference between the person who gives sermons like this and a tape recorder? They only 'learn and sing.' Just by learning cooking, will hunger be appeased? To appease hunger, one has to cook and eat. Disciplined penance is what is essential. That will cultivate good qualities and positive tendencies in us. What is most important is purity and concentration of the mind.

"Amma is not saying that we do not need scriptural study, but scriptural study must be accompanied by spiritual practices. Sadhana is more important. We should not allow a break in that. Like brushing our teeth and taking a bath, Sadhana should become a part of our behavior. Therefore, when a spiritual seeker interacts with worldly affairs, he should be extremely alert."

53. THE ROAD OF DEVOTION, AND THE LIGHT OF KNOWLEDGE

"A vehicle requires headlights to travel on roads in the night. Like that, to travel on the road of devotion, the light of knowledge is required."

- Amma

What one needs is devotion coupled with knowledge. Let us examine some of what Amma shares about this.

"What is knowledge? It is the realization that it is the one God that permeates all beings. Once we understand this, we will not be able to reject anything, we will only accept everything. In our current devotion, we go and tell God about our problems, seeing him as someone separate from us, as someone who gives us everything that we need. We should evolve from this kind of prayer. Our prayer should be, 'Let there be peace, contentment, and happiness for all beings all over the world.' Only then will our devotion be one established in true knowledge instead of selfishness.

"Doesn't Amma say that circumambulating a temple three times, praying, then kicking the beggar who asks for alms saying, 'Get out of the way', can never be called devotion. It is possible that if we give beggars money, they may spend it on drugs or cigarettes. On the other hand, if we give him some clothes to wear, or food to eat, then we can say that our devotion is on the right track. Not only that, from this action we will receive visible satisfaction as well as inner benefit."

Amma herself is the ultimate example of pure devotion. Amma showers love on birds and animals, plants, trees, and even those who oppose her or insult her. Amma sees others in herself, and herself in others. This is devotion is combined with knowledge.

"That is why Amma says that knowledge becomes complete only when one understands one's own Self. The desire for knowledge is inherent in humans. From the day we are born we are engaged in the effort to know about everything around us. We see creation as two-- me, and that which is not me. Meaning, me and the world. We only try to learn about the world, about the external objects. We make no attempt to study ourselves. Due to this we are unable to have a true awareness about life. We are losing ourselves.

"A man would regularly transport a bag of sand on a motorcycle across the border of his state. The policeman on duty would stop him every time and ask him what was in the sack, 'It is only sand sir', the man would reply. "Only sand?" the policeman would ask, "Not drugs, marijuana, gold or something else?' Each time the man would reply boldly, 'No way! It is only sand sir. If you like you may open the sack and inspect it.' To get rid of his doubt, the policeman would open the sack and inspect the contents thoroughly. Once he was sure the sack contained only sand, the policeman would let the man go. Like this, every week, the man would come that way on a motorcycle with a sack of sand. Each time the policeman would let him pass after examining the sack thoroughly. Eventually he stopped coming that way.

"After some time, the policeman entered a hotel to have some food. He saw the man who used to transport the sand, sitting and eating. The policeman approached him and said, 'You are concealing something. Sand is everywhere. So, it is not just sand you were transporting. My mind says that you were definitely smuggling something else across the border. I have no idea what else it could be, though. Because of these thoughts, I can't even sleep well at night. Tell me the truth, what were you smuggling? I will not tell anyone.' Laughing, the man said, 'Sir, I was not transporting sand, but stolen motorcycles.'

"Since the policeman always paid attention only to the sand, he was not suspicious about the motorcycle. Similarly, because we always focus only on the outer world, and external objects, we are unable to study or know ourselves. We forget ourselves. We are unable to know our limitations and shortcomings. Without knowing ourselves we cannot resolve our problems properly. This is because the root cause of all our problems is within ourselves.

"This is why Amma says that spirituality is the knowledge of one's own self. It is the science that can awaken the infinite potential locked in the human mind. In addition to material progress, spirituality trains the mind to experience peace and contentment in any circumstance of life. No matter how much we may grow materially, how much money and position we may have, no one can experience complete peace and happiness with just that alone. Aiming for this is like trying to roll up the sky and place it under the arm. Bliss is within us. It is an attitude of the mind. It is possible to awaken this through spiritual practices. Then, we will be able to understand the nature of the world properly and recognizing what life is. We will be able to manage its gross and subtle aspects appropriately.

"We have heard the stories of those who lived in gold-plated, air-conditioned palaces committing suicide. If you think you can live a problem-free life by making appropriate changes to the external world, it is not possible. It is the mind that we should be 'air-conditioning,' Spirituality is the way to do this. Spirituality is the principle that brings equanimity of mind.

"When we feel the heat inside the house increasing, we go and sit outside in the breeze, or under a tree. When the heat increases outside, we come and sit inside a room with a fan. When we absorb spirituality, we will be able to adjust ourselves to life's circumstances. We will be able to accept the people we come across at their respective levels and move forward with an even mind. Like this we will become victorious both in the external and internal world.

"Today our mind is stuck on material things. It is filled with selfishness. Thus, there is no place for God to reside in us. It is to gain a pure mind, free from all these and to install God within us, that we go to Gurukulas and take refuge in Gurus. But even if we go to such places, these days we pray for wealth. We will say things like, 'I love God,' and so on. But we should be willing to surrender the things that our mind is attached to. Only then will we be able to recognize the real love within us.

"A girl sent her friend a letter on her birthday, 'When I heard it was your birthday, I was so overjoyed I forgot myself. Do you know where all I looked to find you the best birthday gift? Finally, I saw it in a store, but it cost 10 whole rupees. So, I did not buy it. I thought I would save it for another occasion.' What boundless love for her friend! She had once told her that she would even give up her life for her. But she could not spend 10 rupees for her. This is how our love and devotion for God is, we verbally say that we have surrendered everything to God. We promise coconut offerings at the temple to get our work fulfilled. Once the work is done, we buy the smallest, least expensive coconut to offer God.

"Children, none of this is real devotion or love. We should have the attitude of offering even our lives for God. When we offer anything with this attitude, the benefit is for us only. Thinking the other way is like collecting water from a well, taking it to the river and saying, 'O river, aren't you thirsty, here, drink this water.' God does not need anything from us. It is God who gives us everything we require. It is God who purifies us. We get purified through proximity with God.'

"Children, only a mind that has awareness of Dharma (right conduct) can experience the presence of God. What were the people in the olden days like? They were willing to give up their lives even for a fledgling bird. It is this consciousness that brings us closer to God, to the supreme Self. It is an expansive mind that draws us closer to God's presence and lets the divine qualities reflect in us. A mind with this moral consciousness will foster the divine goodness within us. Good actions, good qualities are like the fertilizer that helps a seed grow into a tree. God's grace can never reach a mind filled with selfishness. To be eligible to receive God's grace, we should discard selfishness. Righteous conduct is the way to achieve this.

"In the same way that we get ten seeds when we plant one seed in the ground, if we surrender one to God, we receive a thousand in return from Him. God is the power that protects us. He is not someone that we need to protect. We should understand this. Even if we cannot surrender our mind or body, can't we surrender our desires to God? First offer the selfishness that prevents you from doing this. Is there any necessity to carry the luggage on your head once you have boarded the train? Put the luggage down. The train will carry that load to the destination. If you cannot unburden what is in your head, then you will have to bear the burden yourself.

"Once we have faith in God, then the attitude of surrender should grow. Only then will we get peace and contentment. As long as one remains selfish, each person will have to bear their own burdens. God is not responsible for this. It is not enough to just believe in the doctor. The disease can be cured only if we take the medicine regularly and follow other restrictions. Similarly, it is only when we live according to the divine principles that we become free of the disease of transmigration and reach the goal."

54. HUMILITY IN EVERYTHING

"When an important person is invited to a program, he may receive a nice welcoming ceremony. However, the driver who got that person there may or may not be shown respect by the organizers. Either way the driver does not complain. Likewise, what is working through us is God. It is that energy that the world worships and respects. One should not have any complaints with that."

- Amma

We know that when a driver takes an important personage like a minister, collector, or some other VIP to some place, he does not receive the same treatment as the VIP. The driver, however, does not complain about this or feel sad thinking about it. Because the driver knows, 'The public is admiring the capabilities or the position of the person I just drove here. I don't have that. Then why should I think about it and feel sad or complain?' However, we tend to brag about our capabilities and take on the glory. We proudly say that it is 'my' capability without recognizing that it was given by God.

Amma talks about how we take prideful ownership of our capabilities, without understanding that they have been given by God.

"Once a temple festival procession was going out. The replica of the deity was mounted on a bull. It was walking slowly among the people. The people offered Puja with flowers and performed Arati (waving of sacred flame). Receiving all this and moving forward, the bull thought, "The people worship me so much. I can do anything, and my owner will not be able to do anything to me.' He stopped right there, without moving any further. Seeing this the people began to push the bull. It refused to budge. The owner then took a whip and started flogging it. Only then did the bull realize that the people did not love him, but the deity that was placed on his back. This is our mental state as well.

"When faced with challenges we all have thought, 'I wish someone was here to help me.' These situations cause even atheists to inadvertently remember God. However, unlike many people's perception, divine power is not separate from us. It is a power that is inherent in us. If we pray with the right attitude, we can awaken that power whenever we want.

"In reality, what is prayer? What is the basic principle behind it? Humility is the essence of prayer. We will understand this if we examine the prayer of followers from any religion. 'Dear God, you are omnipotent. Omniscient. I am nothing. I know nothing. So, please protect me.' Isn't this the essence of every prayer? This is a state where we stand humbly in surrender, with bowed head in front of the supreme universal power with the firm conviction, 'I am nothing, you are everything.' This is the correct mental attitude. When we bow low in front of the deity in the sanctum sanctorum of a temple, the thought, 'I am nothing,' should be firmly established in our heart.

"Yet often, bowing down becomes a mere physical gesture. Actions limited to just the body will lack depth. It will not bring the desired results. This is the case with prayer also. When the body is bowing with humility, while the mind is full of arrogance, it is not possible to know or experience divine power. For that, sincere humility is needed. When water falls on top of a mountain it will automatically flow down. God's grace is also like this. Wherever there is humility, God's grace will effortlessly reach there. No matter how strong a gust of wind, it cannot uproot a clump of grass that stays close to the ground. But that same wind uproots big strong trees. Likewise, a humble person can overcome any challenge.

"Practicing humility is difficult for a lot of people. Yet, the truth is that all these good qualities are present within us. They manifest in many situations. For example, don't we listen with, at least external humility, when our bosses or teachers scold us? Don't parents forgive their children's faults and tantrums? To a certain extent, this is done out of helplessness. Yet, such experiences show us that it is possible if we want it. Though we are unaware of it, this obedience and humility is helping us grow.

"Contrary to what we think, the human lifespan is not that long. Time is infinite. In it, 90 or 100 years are like small bubbles that last for a few minutes only. We will recognize this truth if we reflect on it. Before we can shut and open our eyes, childhood, youth, adulthood, and old age come and go, before we blink even once. The Truth of Death, which kicks away everything, is always staring us. If we contemplate this, our arrogance will automatically subside. Humility will happen spontaneously.

"A father and son are playing chess. In the end the father loses the game. Then the son says arrogantly, 'I won! These white chess pieces of mine have a special power.' Putting away the pieces in a box, the father replies, 'Son, no matter whether they are white or black, they all finally go back into the same box. It is possible that the next time, I will be the one that plays with the white pieces, isn't it?' Life is also like this. 'I am great. I am strong. I am rich. I am beautiful.' We live filled with these arrogant thoughts. We forget the divine power that controls everything. We forget the truth that death can happen at any time. We forget our fellow beings, nature, and other living beings. We bow and prostrate to God in front of others, but we forget that the only way to receive God's grace is to have humility, love, and compassion. Children, make humility a habit. That is the best way to make our minds expansive, to develop knowledge and discrimination, and above all to receive God's blessings.

"I am reminded of a story. One day a king felt that he should visit the deity in a distant temple on the next full moon day. After telling his minister, he forgot all about it. On the day before the full moon, the minister approached the king and reminded him of the time for the procession. The next day when the king came out and looked, the streets were full of people. Garlands and other decorations had been put up along the road to welcome him. All the arrangements for the royal visit to the temple and the return journey had been done with great beauty and attention to detail.

"The king's servants and subjects had spared no effort to make his visit to the temple grand. The reason everyone had the energy and enthusiasm to arrange all this, at such short notice, was the king. But the king himself was not part of any of this. The minister had taken the king's permission, and everyone had followed the minister's instructions to the letter. Had the minister made the preparations for this kind of a celebration as an ordinary subject, he would not have been so successful. Each one of us is like this. All our abilities are the abilities of God himself. We are trying to convert those into our capabilities!"

55. WHEN WE POINT OUT UNRIGHTEOUSNESS

"The owner of the vehicle going over the speed limit has to pay a fine. When the fear of paying this fine is not there, accidents and resulting deaths will increase. Likewise, it is when we question unrighteousness in the present moment that we avoid potential harmful results for us and society in the future."

- Amma

It is when we question the unrighteousness that we see in front of us that both we and society are spared from the negative results that could happen in the future. We should definitely point out unrighteous actions when we see them, otherwise they can prove dangerous for us as well as others.

While traveling on the highway, we often drive over the speed limit. It is to control such driving that traffic cameras have been installed. This way both vehicle owners and pedestrians are spared potential accidents. Most ordinary people, who live subject to the control of the mind, are not interested in walking on the path of dharma; most of the time they refrain from wrongdoing out of fear of possible punishment.

In a democracy, one of the reasons the ruling party governs well is out of fear of the opposition. If there is any misconduct, the opposition will bring it to light. This helps the nation to uphold dharma, so that good actions can be done for society.

In this context I am reminded of a scene from the Mahabharata. Since almost everyone knows the story, I will describe it briefly. In the royal gathering where the King Dhritarashtra, Bheeshma, Dronacharya and such dignitaries were present, seeing Dushashana disrobing Panchali, neither King Dhritarashtra, grand sire Bheeshma, nor the Rajguru Dronacharya, who had trained both the Pandavas and the Kauravas in archery, uttered a single word in protest. Had one of them stopped this adharma (moral misconduct) or punished the perpetrators, perhaps the Mahabharata war could have been avoided. What we can infer from this is that the reason for a great war like the Mahabharata was because no one stopped that one act of adharma (unrighteous act) at the right time.

Amma says, "It is only because of the police station and courts that people try, somewhat, to live like good human beings. If someone tries to assault a lady on a bus, just standing by and watching is unrighteous. If no one acts against this, then the very harmony of society is disturbed." Amma is teaching us that pointing out unrighteous acts is in itself rightful conduct.

"Man cannot live without desires. However, desires should be rooted in dharma. Righteous living is essential to maintain the harmony of society and nature. This is possible only if we absorb spiritual principles. The roads have been built for vehicles to drive on. But there is right way to do this. The traffic rules should be obeyed. The speed must be controlled. Forgetting all this, if we drive competing against each other, it will end in an accident. That will affect others as well as ourselves. So, people who break the rules have to pay a fine. It is essential that they are punished. Only then can rightful order prevail on the roads. Only then can there be safety for us and others.

We are the ones who cultivate both righteousness and unrighteousness in our mind. Between these, whichever we nourish is the quality that will flourish.

"The root cause for all the injustices, criminal acts, and problems that we see happening around us is man allowing space in his mind for unrighteous thoughts. If we encourage good thoughts, they will flourish and grow in our minds. Then, love, compassion, and patience will grow in our hearts, and there will be peace and contentment in society.

"Love, compassion, and patience should become our nature. For this we should remove the weeds of arrogance, selfishness, attachment, and hatred from the garden of our minds. We should observe each of our thoughts carefully, discard harmful thoughts and cultivate good thoughts. Think of how much it hurts when someone gets angry at us. Not a single person should be hurt because of us. How happy we are when someone behaves lovingly with us! We should be able to give that happiness to others also. If we have this attitude, we will be able to respond correctly to every situation. The very foundation of life is love, patience, and discrimination. This is what we need more than education or wealth. If we have this, we will be able to achieve everything else. Without understanding this truth, man is creating hell on this heavenly earth. It is our mind that turns this earth into heaven or hell. We ourselves, our minds, are the darkness and light on our path.

"The Rishis did not try to create a separate section of humanity. They used to pray, 'Let everyone be healthy, let everyone be peaceful, let everyone be complete, let everyone have auspiciousness.' From this perspective, when someone commits an unrighteous act, both the perpetrator and the victim, must suffer. To prevent this, we must point out Adharma (unrighteousness) when we see it.

56. THE APPROPRIATE SPIRITUAL PRACTICE

"The decision that vehicles should travel only at such and such a speed on a road is based on the condition of the road. Like this, it is based on the mental state of the disciple that such and such a spiritual practice is advised by the Guru."

- Amma

We often seen sign posts placed along roads which inform us what speed we should drive at, dependent on the condition of the road. Depending on whether the road is winding or steep, near a school or a busy area, whether it is a wide road or a narrow one, we see various speed limits such as 10 km, 60 km, or 100 km written on the road signs. It is like this when a disciple depends on a Guru. The Guru advises him to do such and such spiritual practice, after understanding his mental maturity, past life imprints, and innate tendencies towards action. Even the disciple himself will not be able to comprehend the reasons for specific advice received from the Guru. It is not necessary for the disciple to worry, thinking 'Why did the Guru advise him in this way, but that other fellow in another way.'

Amma says, "Once a disciple joined a Guru's ashram. Before joining the ashram, he had learned how to take videos and photographs at a high level and had gained great expertise. The disciple thought, 'I will be the one to take videos and photos for all the Guru's programs. Then I can always stand near the Guru and do Seva (selfless service).' However, the Guru gave this disciple Seva in the ashram cowshed. There his Seva was to bathe the cows, feed them, milk them, scrape the cow manure, and clean the shed. The disciple who had never done anything like this in his entire life was confused. He thought, Maybe the Guru does not know about my qualifications,' and he took all the certificates he had earned and gave them to the Guru. He then said, 'I have gone to all these places and earned my degrees in all these subjects before coming here. I can do all these things well.'

"The Guru replied, 'I knew very well that you knew all this even before you told me. Now you must learn something that you do not know. That is, you should know the hunger of creatures, which is why I charged you with feeding the cows. Then you must scoop up the manure, only then will you lose your aversion for it. And, only when you milk the cow and give it to others will your selfishness reduce, and your heart become expansive. Just like the cow gives its milk to others, you too should give the fruits of your hard work to others. Only then will there be place in your heart for God'. When the disciple became aware of his mistake, he prostrated to the Guru, returned to the cowshed, and resumed his Seva with happiness and enthusiasm.

Sometimes in the beginning, the Guru will not allow certain disciples to meditate or perform other spiritual practices. They will not have the inner Sattvic qualities (harmony) necessary for this. If such people sit to meditate, they will become drowsy and descend into Tamas (inertia). Understanding this Tamasic nature, the Guru may advise them to perform Karma Yoga (selfless action). Through this, after some time, inner purification happens, removing the Tamas. Only then will the Guru will advise the appropriate spiritual practice slowly. Without understanding this, the disciple may think, 'The Guru has advised the person who came after me to sit for sadhana (meditation, prayer etc.) but makes me perform only karma (action). Why is the Guru being so partial?' This kind of thinking is an expression of his ignorance. The disciple does not know the number of tests that the Guru will guide him through, in order to carve out the perfect disciple.

"Once a Guru gave a disciple a large stone and asked him to sculpt a nice statue from it. The obedient disciple gave up food and sleep, quickly sculpted a statue and offered it at the Guru's feet. He then stood aside with bowed head and folded hands. The Guru glanced at the statue, then picked it up and flung it far away. It shattered into several pieces. 'Is this how you sculpt a statue?' asked the Guru angrily. The disciple looked at the statue and thought to himself, 'I gave up food and sleep, and worked so hard to make this statue, and not a good word.'

"Understanding the disciple's mind, the Guru gave him another stone. Once again, he asked for a statue to made and brought to him. The disciple took the stone and went on his way. With great attention, he made a statue that was even more beautiful than the previous one. He approached the Guru with it. He thought the Guru would definitely like this one. However, the Guru's face turned red when he saw the statue. He said, 'Are you making fun of me? This statue is even worse than the first one.' This one he also threw and broke. The Guru looked at the disciple's face. The disciple was standing with his head bowed, with great humility. Even though he did not harbor feelings of revenge, he did feel sad inside.

"The Guru gave him a stone once more. Again, he asked him to sculpt a statue from it and come back. The disciple left. He fashioned yet another statue with a lot of care. It was an extremely beautiful statue. Again, he offered the statue at his Guru's feet. The Guru threw and broke it, even before he had set it down. He scolded the disciple soundly. This time the disciple did not feel any vengeance or sadness at the Guru's actions. He thought to himself, 'If this is the will of the Guru, let it be so. Any action of my Guru is only for my own good.' The disciple had this attitude of surrender.

"The Guru gave him yet another stone. The disciple accepted it happily. The disciple returned with an extremely beautiful statue; the Guru broke this one also. But there was no change in the disciple's attitude. The Guru was pleased. He embraced the disciple. Placing his hand on his head, he blessed him. 'You have been sculpting the statue within yourself all these days. The stones I gave you were only textbooks for that.'

"If a third person had been observing the actions of the Guru, he might think how cruel he was. He might even think the Guru is crazy. However, only the Guru and the surrendered disciple knew what was happening. Every time the Guru threw the statue and broke it, he was in fact carving out the real statue in the heart of the disciple. What broke was the disciple's arrogance. Only a Satguru is capable of doing this. Only a real disciple can enjoy that bliss.

"The disciple should understand that, more than himself, the Guru is able to know what is good for him and bad for him, what he needs and what he does not need. We should never approach the Guru for name and fame, but only with the goal of surrendering ourselves. If he feels angry when the Guru does not praise his actions, the disciple should see that he has not yet earned the qualifications to be a disciple. He should pray to God for the removal of that resentment. He should be able to see that any action of the Guru is for his own good.

If the disciple leaves the Guru because he thinks he does not get enough praise for his work, the door to the world of eternal bliss is shutting in front of him. It is because the Guru know that patience and maturity cannot be acquired by meditation alone, that he gives his disciples tasks. The good qualities acquired through meditation should be made visible in the disciple's actions. Feeling peace during meditation and agitation once meditation is over is not a sign of true spirituality. He should be able to see any action as meditation. Then action is no longer mere action, it is a meditation. The Guru gives the disciple the appropriate spiritual practices after understanding his mental and intellectual level."

57. IMMERSED IN MEDITATION

"Just as we pay careful attention when we drive on crowded roads, we have to be careful not to let our thoughts wander to other things during meditation."

- Amma

When we drive through a crowded city, we pay extra attention. Because if we are even a little distracted, an accident can take place. In such places, there will be other vehicles in front of us, behind us and on both sides. As such we will drive very carefully. Like this, if we want to, we can train our mind to be attentive as wcll.

During meditation if we observe ourselves, we will see that our attention wanders all over the place. Usually, it takes a long time before we become aware of this. Why does the mind wander like this? The mind has the habit of going where it thinks it will find happiness. If we are to disengage the mind, we have to make it understand that only sorrow will be obtained there. Not just that, we should also teach the mind where it can get true happiness. Only then will the mind withdraw from external objects.

Let us see what Amma has to say about the importance of Shraddha (focused attention): "Meditation is like unearthing a precious gemstone. The mind that is pulled outwards is going to pick up shining pieces of glass instead. When we carry these glass pieces around, our hands can get cut, and the bag we carry these glass pieces in can also tear. If we constantly train the mind to think like this, then it will slowly attain Shraddha.

"Once the Guru in an ashram told the disciple, 'You should watch that your thoughts do not flow outward. You should try to keep your mind introverted.' The disciple replied, 'I am unable to do this, O Guru, what should I do?' The Guru said matter-of-factly, 'Come with me.' Saying this he took the disciple and went out into the field to the rabbit cage. He instructed the disciple to open the cage. The disciple did, and the rabbits jumped out and ran in all directions. Then the Guru said, 'Now put all the rabbits back in the cage.' The disciple tried, but no matter what he did, he was unable to put all the rabbits back into the cage. Finally, the disciple surrendered, saying, 'Guru, I cannot do this.' 'Here, let me show you how,' said the Guru. Saying this, the Guru let the ashram dog out of his cage. As soon as they saw the dog, all the rabbits quickly scurried into their cage. The Guru said, 'The mind is like this. When it thinks that happiness is in the external world, it runs after objects. However, knowing that these objects bring only sorrow is dispassion. Once dispassion awakens, our mind will automatically refrain from flowing outwards. Such a mind will be introverted and will quickly get the concentration for meditation. Once the mind realizes that this introversion will reveal precious gemstones, it will start finding happiness in that.'

"This is the reason that peace and contentment are not found in the majority of people nowadays. They do not know where to find happiness. They build large palaces and commit suicide inside them. If palatial homes, wealth, various comforts, and alcohol gave real happiness, why would people who have these things suffer and die? Happiness is definitely not in any of these things. Peace and contentment depend entirely on our mind. What is this mind? Where is its source? What is the goal of life? What is life? How should one live? None of these are understood. If we understand these things, and live accordingly, then we need not wander anywhere in search of peace. Today everyone is searching for peace and happiness outside themselves.

"Once an old woman was busily searching for something in the front yard of her house. A man passing by asked her, 'Aunty, what are you searching for?' She said, 'I lost my earrings. I am searching for them.' To help the woman, the man too began searching in the front yard. No matter how much they searched, they could not find the earrings. The man asked her, 'Do you remember where exactly your earrings fell?' The old woman replied, 'Son, the earrings fell somewhere inside the room.' Hearing her reply the man became angry, 'Instead of searching in the room where you lost them, how do you expect to find them out here?' The old lady replied, 'Son, what nonsense are you talking? It is dark inside the room. Here there is light. That is why I am searching here.' We are also like this woman. If we want to experience peace in life, we should understand the real source of happiness, and search for it there. It is not possible to get peace from the external world. Peace and contentment depend on a person's mind.

"Only if we have love for our chosen deity, will its form become clear inside us. We should always have this thought - we are not seeing the image; we are not seeing the image. The attitude a seeker should have towards God is that of a lover to his beloved. We should reach a state where we cannot be without God for even a single moment. That much love should develop. If the lover sees his beloved in a blue sari, then wherever he sees the color blue, he will see his beloved, he will remember her form. Even while eating or sleeping he thinks of her alone. From the time he wakes up in the morning, he dreams of her alone. Even while brushing his teeth, or drinking his morning coffee, he will be wondering what his beloved is doing at that moment. We should have such a love for our chosen deity. It should be impossible to think of anything other than the deity. Even bitter gourd, when steeped in sugar, will become sweet after some time. Similarly, even if our mind is filled with negative thoughts, if we constantly think about God and surrender them to the divine, our minds will become pure.

"One day in Vrindavan, as a gopi (milkmaid) was walking along, she saw a hole under a tree. She began to imagine, 'Krishna must have come this way. The gopi, who was with him, must have told Bhagavan she wanted the flower from the tree nearby. Bhagavan must have held the gopi's shoulders and jumped up onto the tree. This hole in the ground is the imprint of his feet when he jumped.' She calls the other gopis and showed them the hole formed by the imprint of Bhagavan's feet. They forgot everything in the remembrance of Bhagavan. For that gopi everyone standing around transformed into Krishna. When somebody touched her shoulder, she felt it was Krishna himself, and in the ecstasy of devotion she lost consciousness. Those standing nearby also lost external awareness thinking of Krishna. Everyone was shedding tears of bliss in the memory of Bhagavan. We should also have this attitude. See everything as Bhagavan. There is no world without Bhagavan. Such people need not make any special effort to clearly visualize their chosen deity during meditation. Because in their minds, there is no moment when Bhagavan is not present.

"O trees and vines, where is my Mother? O birds and animals, where is my Mother? O ocean, and backwaters, where is the embodiment of power, that mother who gave you the power to exist?' Our mind should cry out like this whenever we see something. We can imagine and cry. As we practice like this, our mind is cutting up each obstacle, and continuously adhering to those divine feet. Imagine like this, it is absolutely possible.

"If we sit down to meditate, saying, 'I will meditate now,' we will not get the form within. We are merely sitting with eyes closed. Only after a long time will we remember to pray, 'Amma, I am sitting down to meditate.' Before sitting for meditation, we should call God and cry, 'God, please come before me. I cannot see you without your help. You alone are my sole refuge.' We should cry out saying this. We should visualize that God is standing in front of us. After a long time, if we start every meditation like this, the form will shine clearly within us."

When that happens, our thoughts will not drift to other objects of the world, and we will be able to meditate successfully.

58. SORROWS THAT HELP US

"When we are driving on a smooth highway there is a greater possibility of nodding off. But when driving through a road with potholes and bumps, there is lesser possibility of sleeping at the wheel. Because the driver will stay alert."

- Amma

"Usually while traveling on a good highway, there will be fewer obstacles. There are no vehicles coming from the other direction. So, driving takes less effort. The only effort is to press the accelerator. As such, there is the possibility of falling asleep at the wheel, especially when travelling at night. This can cause serious accidents. We could lose a limb, or even our life. On the contrary when we drive on country roads, the incessant bumps, potholes, twists, and turns keep us awake. We will constantly be changing gears and applying the brake. We will stay alert. So, there is no chance of carelessness or falling asleep. This will save us from great dangers.

In the Mahabharata there is an instance where Kunti Devi prays to the Lord to always give her sorrow. When asked why, she said that a life not spent always remembering God is like sleeping through life. We often forget to remember God during happy times. But when we have sorrow, we call to God, and he comes running. Kunti Devi's attitude was, 'I always pray for sorrow. In this way I can always have Bhagavan's darshan (vision).' From this we should understand that if we always experience happiness, we may not remember God. It is sorrow that usually makes someone turn towards God.

If we examine the lives of Mahatmas, we can see that sorrows were one of the motivations that got them to Self-Realization. Sorrow should become our Guru. Amma has always considered sorrow to be a light in the darkness. In this world there are so many people who live in depression, unable to manage life's sorrows. Yet, if we direct the sorrows and suffering that life gives us towards the Supreme Self in the form of prayer, sorrow is transformed into the power and light of Divine Love. Perhaps this is why Amma says that sorrow is a Guru for human beings.

Once there was a virtuous householder who was a karma yogi (person with mental discipline). At one point he had to deal with a succession of hardships. One day he sat at home overcome with sorrow. Seeing her husband in the grip of sorrow and depression for the first time, the wife thought about how to help him. She put on black clothes and went and stood in front of her husband. Astonished at this, the husband asked, 'Why are you wearing black clothes?' She replied, 'I want to express my condolences.' Hearing this he asked with some trepidation, 'Who died?' 'God,' the faithful wife said to her puzzled husband. 'As long as God is present within us, we have no reason for feeling disappointment or depression. Since you are now sitting like this, depressed and disappointed, I have concluded that God must have died.' His wife's answer hit him hard. That devout householder came out of his depression, and with God-remembrance continued to engage in his work with self-confidence. As far as a devotee is concerned, feeling depressed is akin to being an atheist.

Let us listen to what Amma has to say in this regard.

"If we selflessly take refuge in Bhagavan, he will provide everything we need at the right time. If we have an attitude of surrender, that he will look after everything, then we need not fear anything. Auspiciousness and happiness will flourish everywhere. If one has innocent devotion, Goddess Lakshmi (Goddess of wealth) will become his servant. Yet, what is our devotion like? We say we are going to the temple. None of us go to the temple simply to see God. Even in front of Bhagavan, we can only talk about worldly things. If we must tell an omniscient God the news about our home and neighborhood, why go to a temple? With the belief that God knows all our problems without us having to tell Him, surrender everything to God, at least when we are at the temple. We should not make God just a complaint box. We should go to the temple to worship God and to sustain that remembrance. Only then will we get the benefit of temple worship.

"If we take proper refuge in God, only goodness will come to us, both materially and spiritually. There is no record of any Mahatma dying from starvation. The three worlds have only prostrated in front of them. No one who has surrendered to God will ever have to experience the sorrow of poverty. The main reason for our sorrows today is that we lack surrender to God. If we are sorrowful today, it only means that we do not have proper submission to God. Our devotion is not for devotion's sake, but for the fulfillment of desires. It is desires which pave the way for sorrow.

"Why should one knowingly fall into a ditch? When we have the means to get rid of sorrow, then why wallow in it? Like the heat of the sun, the coolness of water, joys and sorrows are the nature of life. Then why should we grieve and lose our strength? Why should we work for no wages? If being sad brings results, then be sad. Nonetheless, if the body is wounded, what is required is to apply medicine immediately. There is no use just sitting and crying. If action is not taken, it could get inflamed and septic and could even endanger your life. Similarly, if we understand spirituality, we will not be defeated by trivial challenges. We will be able to overcome them and move forward.

"If we stand in a festival ground knowing that there will be fireworks, we will not be startled by that noise. It is when we stand without knowing, that we are frightened when the Amuttu (string of fireworks with gunpowder) is fired off. We become so scared that we may even fall sick. The way to escape sorrow is to move ahead knowing and focusing on the Self. It is not possible to bring the mind under control in a second. It is difficult to cross the ocean. Yet, one who strives, after learning how to do that, goes across, doesn't he? The Mahatmas have shown us the way to cross this ocean of worldly existence. Those are the scriptures. You only need to live according to those. We should imbibe the true principles by studying the scriptures and listening to Satsangs (spiritual talks). We should never lose an opportunity to be in the company of Mahatmas. We should live applying their teachings in our life. A person who moves with faithful focus will be able to avoid sorrows in life.

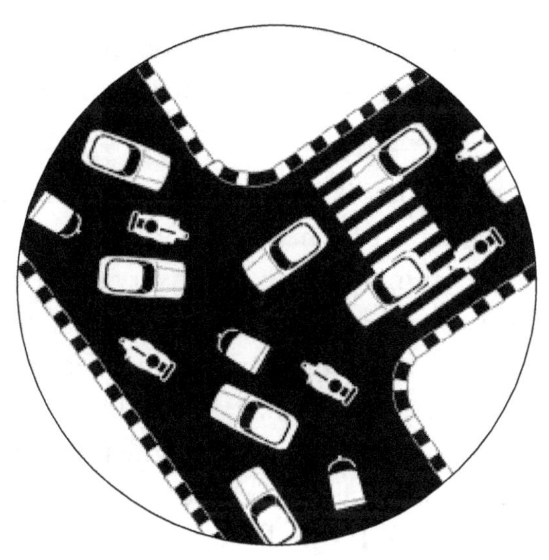

59. WHEN VEDANTA BECOMES LIFE

"When we are learning how to drive a vehicle, we obey the road rules fully. But, after learning, the percentage of people who drive fully following the rules will be very small. Similarly, though there are plenty who have learnt Vedanta, those who actually live practicing it are very few."

- Amma

We all know that when we learn driving, we follow the instructions to the letter. However, after getting the license, only very few people drive according to the rules. For example, in India, while learning to drive, we put our right hand out and make a signal before moving forward. When we want to stop the vehicle, we also show the appropriate signal, which is to put our right hand out, open the palm and wave the hand up and down. Nowadays most of the vehicles are air conditioned. So, how many drivers roll down the window and signal with their hand while driving these days?

Amma says, "This is just like enthusiastically memorizing the Brahmasutra, teaching it to others, yet not being able to realize the knowledge of Brahman, which is the very goal of the Brahmasutra." What we should understand here is that Amma does not acknowledge those who simply study some Vedanta and walk around saying that they are Brahman. This is like saying the seed is Brahman and the tree is Brahman. It is true that the seed contains the tree. Yet, the seed will not be able to give the shade, fruit, and wood that a tree can. It should go beneath the soil, sprout, and grow into a tree. Only then is it beneficial to others. A true Vedantin (who practices Vedanta) does not see anyone as separate from himself. This is because he lives the Vedantic principles.

Let us see what Amma has to say: "The scriptures are not something to be understood only through the intellect. They have to be known through experience. The scriptures are as vast as the ocean. It is not necessary for individuals to know all of that. What we need are the principles in the scriptures. There are like the gems found in the ocean. Those who eat sugarcane only suck out its juice, they spit out the pulp. Only a person who has performed spiritual practices can understand the subtleties of the scriptures and reject what is not necessary for himself.

"No one becomes complete just by studying the scriptures. A person bought medicine to cure his illness. The dosage and instructions on how to take the medicine were written on the bottle. If he just sits there reading, his illness will not be cured. He has to take the medicine. One will not get liberation just by studying the scriptures. Practicing is required as well. Meditation along with scriptural study is much better than meditating without having studied the scriptures. When the mind of a person who has studied the scriptures becomes agitated, instead of being sad, he is able to reflect on the scriptural dictums and gain inner strength. He can then remove his weaknesses. Only a person who has studied the scriptures and performed spiritual practices can serve the world selflessly.

"Scriptural study is essential up to a certain extent. A person who has studied agriculture will have no problem planting and cultivating a plant. He knows the methods and medicines needed to remove any diseases the plant might have. Yet just sitting there drawing a picture of a plant, will not get results. For results we must plant and nurture it. If we want to experience what is described in the scriptures, spiritual practices are required. Amma says that someone who spends time only studying the scriptures without doing sadhana, is like someone who draws the blueprint of a house and tries to live in that. Knowledge of the scriptures is like traveling while knowing the route. The journey will be easy, and we will reach the goal quickly.

"The seed that is lying in the storehouse has the attitude that everything is contained in it. It thinks, 'Why should I bow my head in front of the soil?' It does not think that it will only grow after going underneath the dirt, that lots of fruits and seeds will be produced from it, and that others will also benefit. Like this, it lies in the storehouse and finally gets eaten by cockroaches or rats. Those who only possess scriptural expertise are like these seeds which lie in the granary. They are only capable of repeating, 'I am Brahman', 'I am Brahman,' like a parrot.

"Once a person who had studied the scriptures asked Amma,

'Don't the scriptures say that everything is Brahman (divinity)?' Amma replied, "We have not reached that state. Therefore, we should live using discrimination. Even though we say everything is filled with divinity, it is not good to go stand in front of a rabid dog. The person who stops us from doing this is also Brahman. We should have the discrimination to do what is necessary. Otherwise, our life is wasted.'

"As long as it has not become our experience, what is the point of walking around saying things? We see objects like baskets, winnowing sieves and chairs woven from cane. The cane makes up the baskets, winnowing sieves and chairs. Similarly, the baskets, winnowing sieves and chairs are made up of cane. We should be able to see this. There is gold in the earring, bangle, and ring. Yet those who are deluded by the form will only see the ornaments. Those who are not deluded by form will be able to see the gold as well. Even though the ornaments are different from one another, and are used for different purposes, we should be able to see one gold in all of them. We should develop this vision. We should understand that there is only one truth, one Brahman in everything. Those who are capable of seeing this will not be able to commit wrongs. It is those who only pay lip-service to Brahman, who have not known it at the level of experience, who commit wrongs. Advaita is a state where there are no two. It is a spontaneous state where you can see others as yourself. It is not something to be talked about, it is life itself.

"There was a man who took loans from several people, purchased an island, and lived there in a palatial house he had built. Whenever anyone visited him, all he could talk about was his palace and his greatness. One day a Sannyasi (ascetic) came there to beg alms. The sadhu (ascetic) did not show him enough respect. This angered the rich man. He said to the sadhu, 'Do you know who this island and palace belongs to? Who the owner of all this is? All this belongs to me! I am the only one entitled to all of this. Up until today no one has ever disrespected me like you have.' After listening to everything, the sadhu asked, 'Does all this belong to you? The man replied angrily, 'Yes, all this is mine.' 'Really?' asked the sadhu. 'Yes, it's true,' the man replied. The sadhu looked him in the eye and asked, 'With whose money did you purchase all this? Ask your own conscience this question.'

Hearing this, the rich man felt foolish. He became aware of his mistake. Nothing there was really his. He prostrated at the feet of the sadhu.

"The knowledge that we have today has not been gained by bringing it to the experiential level through sadhana. Without doing sadhana, people sit around saying 'I am Brahman' after reading some books written by others. While saying, 'I am Brahman', they do not have even an iota of compassion towards people. They have no humility, no tolerance. Such people do not have the right to even say the word 'Brahman'.

"If we teach a parrot, it will also say 'Brahmam, Brahmam'. But a cat will only hear, 'kiyo, kiyo'. Crying 'kiyo, kiyo' like this, the parrot will become food for the cat. Therefore, instead of simply saying, 'Brahman, Brahman,' we should imbibe that principle. For this we should contemplate on Brahman every minute and firmly establish it in our mind. That principle symbolizes compassion and expansiveness. Advaita is a state where there is no two. This has to be known at the level of experience.

Those who have experienced Brahman have no need to say, 'I

am Brahman'. We will be able to feel this even if we just go near them. The smile on their face will not fade, whatever the circumstance. Currently our 'Brahman' is like a tree-seed. How will it be if the seed says, 'I am a tree?' When it becomes a tree, we can even tie an elephant to it. If we do not watch the seed, then it becomes food for some birds. That principle is indeed within us. But we should bring this to the level of experience, by cultivating humility and simplicity, and through methods like Svadhyayam (mindful study) and Nididhyasan (sustained meditation on the sacred texts).

60. A MAP CALLED THE SCRIPTURES

"We will reach our destination only if we drive following the directions on the map. Similarly, only if we live according to what the scriptural sciences say can we reach the goal."

- Amma

If we have to go to an unknown place, then someone will look at the address and write down the directions or draw a map on how to reach there. If we just sit there, staring at these directions, we will never reach our destination. Only if we make the journey according to the map will we reach there. The study of scriptural texts is also like this. Just because we have studied these texts does not mean we will attain the goal of life. Only when we live according to the scriptural teachings can we reach that goal

What is spiritual science? It is the experience of the Rishis (ancient sages), who performed intense penance for endless years. What a Self-Realized master says is also scripture. He shares with his disciples how he himself reached the goal. It is not enough to just listen to the Guru. Only when the disciple contemplates deeply on his Guru's words, and lives according to the Guru's teaching, will he attain the goal.

In today's society we can see so many scriptural scholars who are wandering around, without applying the spiritual principles in their lives. This science can give you the ability to preach so that you can earn enough to have food to eat, and clothes to wear. Applying these teachings to life is a penance. Amma says, that, 'such a seeker will not need to wander in search of anything. Whatever they need will reach them where they are. The very presence of such a person will create peace in others.'

Studying the scriptures, and assimilating the teaching are two separate things. We will not get results simply by studying the scriptures. The results will happen only when we assimilate the teachings and live according to them.

Let us see what Amma says about the importance of applying spiritual principles in our lives.

"Our hunger will not be satiated if we only learn how to cook. To enjoy, we must actually cook the food and eat it. It is not enough to just learn agriculture. Only when you plant trees and cultivate them will you get fruits. Just having the information about where to dig to get water is not enough. We must dig there and take the water. Just drawing a picture of a well will not quench your thirst. For that you must dig the well and draw the water from it. It is not enough to sit in a vehicle looking at the map, only if you travel via the route that is on the map, will you reach the destination.

"Similarly, it is not enough for you to just participate in Satsangs (gathering of spiritually minded people) and read scriptural texts. If you want an experience of the Truth, then you should be willing to live according to these teachings. Only when you do spiritual practices will you be able to escape being a victim of circumstances. You must be able to apply the principles that you have understood in your life. Listen to Satsang, and then live the principles. We should take refuge in God with a selfless attitude, shedding all desires.

'I am Brahman', 'Tat tvam asi', although the scriptures proclaim these truths, it is only when inner ignorance is removed that the light of knowledge can shine within. As long as one does not perform sadhana, uttering dictums like 'Aham Brahmasmi', 'Tat tvam asi', is like naming a blind child 'Light.' That child does not even know what light is.

"Once a man was giving a sermon in which he said: 'Aren't we all Brahman. Then why do we need sadhana and all?' After the sermon he came and sat down to eat. The server put a plate in front of him. When he looked, he saw pieces of paper placed on the plate with the names of the dishes written on them-- rice, sambar, toran, payasam... There was nothing to eat. He became angry and said, 'What are you doing? Are you making fun of me?' The server replied, 'Sir, I heard you preach that just the thought that we are Brahman is enough, and that spiritual practices are not required. So instead of eating the food, surely it is enough to think about food. I was sure the very thought would fill your stomach.'

"Children, it is not enough to just preach, you should act. Only through sadhana can you manifest the essence of the teaching. For someone who is not making any effort, listening to Satsang (spiritual talk) is like a fox getting an unhusked coconut. It will not appease his hunger. A tonic is meant to improve the health. The dosage will be written on it. It will help you only if you follow those instructions. Satsangs (spiritual talks) are like understanding the dosage of a tonic and spiritual practice is like drinking it.

"You can understand the difference between the permanent and impermanent from Satsangs, but you can make this your experience only if you do sadhana. When you assemble the various parts needed to make a radio correctly and connect them to the battery, then you can sit at home and listen to the programs being broadcast by the radio station far away. If we tune our mind appropriately, if we lead our lives according to the Mahatmas' instructions, we can experience bliss when we are in this body itself. If we perform sadhana and selfless service, then we do not need anything else.

"No matter how much we may study Vedanta, unless we do spiritual practices, we cannot experience it. What we are searching for exists within us. To attain that we need sadhana. If a seed is to become a tree, it must be planted in the ground, watered, and fertilized. It is not enough to merely hold it in our hand."

61. WHEN THOUGHTS BUILD A NEST ON OUR HEAD!

"Would we allow someone else to leave their car in our car shed? It is like this that we allow thoughts to stay in our mind."

- Amma

When we visit large cities, we may have to drive around for a while without getting a parking spot. However, when we are home, we will not allow another vehicle to park in our garage. If we do that, our own car will have to park somewhere outside. If we park the car of God in the garage of our mind, then the cars of other thoughts will not park there.

Once a man owned an auto-rickshaw. The regular rickshaw driver could not come, so this man hired a new rickshaw driver.

Whenever the new driver drove the rickshaw, he would get fewer fares. When the owner asked why this was happening, the driver said he had no idea. The owner told him that if he stayed in one spot, he would not get passengers. Instead, he should be constantly driving around the city. Only then would people hail him for a ride. The owner decided to accompany him. From the next day onwards, the owner also sat in the rickshaw.

The driver started driving the rickshaw. Even though they drove around till the evening, not a single person approached them. The same thing happened the next day. When reflecting on the possible reasons, the owner understood why no one hailed them. Passengers would see that someone was already sitting in it, so they would think that the auto had already been hired. Thinking this, they would not wave the rickshaw down.

Our mind is also like this. If we cherish one thought in our mind, then other thoughts will not attempt to come and stay there. The reason being that when thoughts look, they won't see any available space in our minds. So, they will go back the same way they came. Many thoughts come and go. We should not give these thoughts space to reside in our mind.

Let us listen to some examples Amma uses to explain this.

"Thoughts are like birds that fly over our head. If we allow them to build a nest on top of our head, then they will become a nuisance for us. A natural question will arise in our mind, 'Is it possible for us to control our minds like this? What Amma says is, 'If we have that supreme love towards God, surely we can do this.'

"Once the devotees in Mathura asked Bhagavan Krishna 'O Bhagavan, you always speak about Radha. Who is she? What does she look like? Till today we have not even seen a painting of her. Would you draw us a picture of Radha so we can see her?' Bhagavan said, 'Okay'. Bhagavan started drawing Radha's picture. After some time when they looked at the picture that Bhagavan had drawn, it was the image of Bhagavan himself. The devotees said, 'We do not want to see your picture, it is Radha's picture we want to see.' Then Krishna said, 'Oh, okay. I must have made a mistake. I will draw another picture right now.' Saying this, Bhagavan again started drawing again. The same thing happened. Instead of Radha's form Bhagavan had drawn his own form. When this repeated several times, the devotees asked, 'Do you not remember Radha's form at all? Aren't you able to realize that you are drawing your own image?' Bhagavan said, 'I am clearly visualizing Radha in my mind's eye while drawing the picture. However, because Radha has completely forgotten herself, and her mind is constantly fixed on me, in her place I can only see my image. What can I do. Radha and Krishna are not two, but one.' In the presence of that supreme love there was no room for separate thoughts.

"Someone who has that kind of longing will not give up thinking of God for even a minute. Food and sleep are not a problem for them. Their hearts will ache with longing, constantly thinking of God."

Listen as Amma describes her girlhood days, when she was overwhelmed with longing for God.

"In childhood, I started searching for God. Until the time I experienced him, I was in agony. There was no time to wipe the endless stream of tears. I would not sleep. When night fell, my heart would throb with pain, 'Has another day gone by? Have

I not wasted yet another day without knowing you?' That pain is unbearable. I would think that if I did not sleep, then that day would not be done, and so I would stay awake all night long. Always searching, 'Where are you? Where are you?' Unable to bear the pain of not seeing God, I would bite my body.

'Sometimes I would roll on the ground. I would chant God's name and cry out loud. Without knowing why, I would burst into tears. At other times I would not even feel like smiling. 'A smile that does not know God, what kind of a smile is that? Without knowing you, why should I be happy? Why should I even eat food without knowing you or take a bath?' This was how I got through each day.

"When one develops intense dispassion, one feels aversion towards the world. Yet one should cross that stage also. We should be able to see everything as God. Other thoughts are like fragments of glass. When we pick them up, our hand gets cut. The bag we place those in, also tears. Like this if we teach our mind that it is full of danger, then through practice, the mind will not let other thoughts have any room to stay."

62. THE IMPERMANENCE OF WORLDLY COMFORTS

"Sometimes we travel in air-conditioned luxury buses. But we still get down when it reaches our destination. We do not keep sitting in the bus saying it is nice to sit there. Like this, in life we have used nice things, have had high positions. But we should understand that God is our true goal and be willing to relinquish our luxuries at any given moment for that."

- Amma

While traveling by a luxury bus, we may have thought about how many conveniences and comforts the bus has, how plush the seats are! We may not even feel like leaving the bus. Yet when the journey is over, we will not continue to sit in the bus. For the sake of the goal, we are prepared to give up these comforts. Similarly for the sake of Self-realization, the goal of life, when required, we should always be ready to give up high status, loving relationships, and expensive objects.

Only if we leave the place we are sitting on, can we travel to the next place. Externally we should be prepared to give up whatever relationships we have with anyone, all our mental bonds. We should understand that these people will not always be with us, and certainly not come with us at the end of our lives. It could be said that relationships are like passengers who are traveling together with us on a train. While traveling by train, many people come and sit next to us. We get to know them. It is possible that we may even establish a close bond with them. But they may not be with us till we reach our destination. When they reach their station, they will get up and leave.

"If we understand this, we will not have to grieve. Before people leave us, we should be mentally prepared to give them their freedom. If we fix our gaze on the goal of Self-realization, then renouncing all these bonds will not be difficult. This is also the case with status and position. No matter what the status, at some point we will have to let go of it. No position in life is permanent. If we think we will stay in that one position throughout our lives, then we will have to suffer. Therefore, without wasting our life only for name and fame, we must do what we must do, anchored in dharma (right moral conduct), and keep progressing towards the goal of realizing God. If we must relinquish our position for this, we should be ready for that also.

This is also the case with our money and other valuable possessions. We should always be aware that none of these are permanent. The fortune that is in our hands today, could belong to someone else tomorrow. At any time, expensive things can be destroyed. So, we should not waste our life in their pursuit alone, thinking all this to be true and permanent. We should be ready to renounce all of this at any time for the goal of God-realization.

The next attachment to consider is that to our body. Why do we develop this attachment? It is because of ignorance. A realized Mahatma knows that 'I am not this perishable body', but the Self, which is the embodiment of awareness. Yet the ignorant one is firmly entrenched in the belief that, 'I am the body.' This is why in the Mahabharata it is said that the biggest wonder in the world is that even though we see people, and other creatures around dying daily, we think we will not die. It is certain that one day we will have to leave this body. When that time comes, we will not have the power to retain the body for even an extra minute. We should put in the effort to know who we are before we leave the body. For this we should always be prepared to bid farewell to anything that we consider as good in our lives.

If we remain attached to the happiness and comforts that have come our way due to God's blessings, which are nevertheless temporary, we will never reach the goal.

Let us see how Amma clarifies this point.

"Children, we have received this human body so that we may use it to strive for God-realization. With each passing day, we come closer to death. When we enjoy material pleasures, the power within us is slowly draining away. Yet the more we meditate on God, the stronger the mind become and the more positive tendencies we develop. Like this we can overcome even death. Therefore, we should try to attain victory over our weaknesses when we are young and healthy. Then we need not fear thinking about tomorrow, and we will not fear today.

There was a country where any of the citizens could become the king. However, there was one condition. He could be king only for five years. After that he would be taken and left on a deserted island nearby. It only had a forest filled with cruel, wild animals. The wild animals would kill and eat whoever reached that island. Even though they knew about this, many citizens continued to come forward to become king, driven by the desire to enjoy the kingly comforts and powers. When they would ascend the throne, they would all be happy. But soon afterwards, the fear of becoming prey to the wild animals, made them sad all the time. Their faces were always gloomy. Enthusiasm left them. They had good food, luxurious comforts, servants, dances by dancers, yet they were not interested in anything. From the time they became king, they lived each day seeing death in front of them.

"Those who had come to enjoy, were not free from sorrow for even for a single moment. They were unable to open their hearts to become involved in anything. One day after the most recent king's time was over, he was left at the island and became a meal for the animals. After this another young man came forward to become king. But the new king was not like the others. After he became king, he did not become sad like the previous ones. He would laugh with everyone, dance, go horseback riding and hunting, ask about the citizen's welfare, and look after the matters of the country. He was always happy.

"Finally, his days were also coming to an end. Still there was no change of expression on his face. Everyone was astonished. They asked him, 'Your highness, the day for you to go to the island is nearing. Yet we do not see any sorrow in you. The others were not like this. From the time they ascended the throne, they would be anxious about death. You, however, are joyful both then and now'.

"The king replied, 'Why should I be unhappy? I am prepared to go to the island. There will be no wild animals there to kill and eat me. As soon as I became king, I learned how to hunt. Then I took soldiers to the island and hunted down all the cruel animals. I cut down the forests and converted it into farmland. I dug wells and had various buildings constructed and appointed servants. I selected some poor people who had no land of their own, and gave them land on the island, a means of livelihood, and settled them there. They love me as the visible form of God. I too want to spend the rest of my life there, happily working on the farm, loving the flowers, butterflies, and birds. Even though I will be giving up the throne, I can live there just like a king. Everything I need is already there.'

"Amma says, children, we should also be like this king. We should be able to find that abode of eternal bliss even while living in this material world. However, now we are like the first kings. We are filled with anxiety and tension thinking about tomorrow. Because of that we are unable to fulfill today's responsibilities properly. Sorrow today, sorrow tomorrow. There is not a single day free of tears till the end of our lives. On the other hand, if we spend each moment of the present day with attention, then we will not have to worry tomorrow. Our days will be filled with happiness.

"Children, we should not think, 'Let us enjoy the material world now, and then later we can think about God.' Materialism will never give us complete satisfaction. We may feel satiated after eating some milk pudding. Yet, after some time we will feel like eating twice that amount. So, do not ever wait to be satisfied by the material world to call on God. If you are thinking, 'Let me experience this one desire first, you will never be satisfied.' Desires are not something that will get destroyed like that. Only one who has renounced desires can become complete. Perform your duties with a mind that is surrendered to God. Then we can even overcome death. We can live joyfully."

63. ORGAN DONATION

"We recycle the nuts and bolts and other spare parts from a damaged vehicle to use in other vehicles. Similarly, it is a laudable thing to donate our organs to others when we die."

- Amma

Even when a vehicle breaks down, many of its parts are still usable. These kinds of usable parts can be taken out and used in other vehicles. Right from the nuts, bolts and tires, many parts can be reused. By doing this not only are we reducing expenditure, but we are also maximizing the utility of the vehicle's parts.

The human body is also like this. After brain death, so many of the body parts can be donated. Eyes, liver, nose, heart, arms, and legs, and many more body parts can be transplanted into another human being.

In the examples below, Amma emphasizes the value of donating one's organs after death.

"If we cremate the body, it gets reduced to ashes. If we bury it, it becomes food for the worms. Yet if we donate our organs to others, many of our main organs will continue to live through many others. We will live on in the minds of the organ recipients and their loved ones. Our organs can give sight to someone, sometimes even the gift of life itself.

"It is a good thing to donate our organs after death. Children, you should think about the happiness of the recipient patient when his life is saved through the donation of a new heart, liver, or kidney. You should imagine how the blind man, who is able to see through the donation of a pair of eyes, will rejoice along with his family. This can save all of them from a life of misery. This does good not only for the person who donates the organs, and the one who receives them, but also for the soul of the donor."

Amma goes on to describe how the doctors at the ashram's super specialty hospital AIMS in Kochi were able to use all the organs donated by someone to save others' lives. The organs were donated by one of the father of one of the doctors.

"When he was healthy, he left signed papers at AIMS declaring his wish to be an organ donor. Before cremating the body, the doctor removed all his father's organs. The choice of organ donation showed that he knew what the body is, what happens to it after death, and how valuable the organs of the body are. It a testament to the fact that, 'You are not the body, when you have your organs donated after death. Never while you are alive! Why should you grieve thinking about what is happening to the body after death? You yourself have chosen a life of sacrifice, surrender and service of others.'

Amma also says, "The body is the cause of all sorrow. The body is a bundle of sorrow born as the result of prior actions. We perform each action based on our infatuation with the sense of pride in the 'I" and arrogance. Arrogance arises from the delusion of ignorance. Due to the connection with Maya, one has the delusional notion that one is the body. It is this thought that traps a person in worldly life. Because of this, the mind cannot reach the path to liberation.

"According to the levels of merits and demerits, of the good and bad deeds done by each person, he is reborn in either a higher class or lower-class family and continues to experience the effects of his karma. Karma (action) is the cause for rebirth, regardless of whether it is meritorious or sinful. Some people perform charity and fire sacrifices because they desire to live in heaven. When they reach heaven after death, they can live there happily only as long as the merit from their previous good deeds remains. Once the merit is over, they fall from the Chandra Mandala (lunar sphere), merge with the mist and fall to earth. There they become paddy and other grains, which are eaten by man and transformed into blood. Then it becomes semen and is embedded in the womb of a woman. The sac in the womb immediately envelops, it and it is mixed with the blood in the womb.

"In one day, the semen and blood are mixed and becomes an embryo. When five nights are over, it swells into the shape of bubbles. Then, in another five days it gets enveloped in small drops of blood. After twenty-five days, small growths of organs start sprouting here and there. In three months, the limbs parts develop joints, and in the fourth month fingers emerge. In the fifth month, teeth, nails, genitals, nose, eyes, and ears form. In the sixth month the ears develop opening. The genital organs, the loins, the excretory organs, and mouth form in the seventh month. In the eighth month, hair starts growing on the head and body. In the ninth month the fully grown fetus in the womb starts moving its arms and legs. From the fifth month itself the life force starts expressing itself in the child. The child's umbilical cord draws the essence of the food consumed by the mother and brings it to the child's body to sustain it.

"As soon as body is nourished and the life force is established, the child remembers its past life. 'God, in how many wombs have I taken birth. How many evil deeds have I done. How much money did I earn by unfair means. At that time, I did not practice God-remembrance or chanting. Dear God, it is the fruit of these actions that I am experiencing now. When will I be able to come out of this hell? After I am born, I will not commit any evil acts. I will do only good deeds with all my strength!' Like this, thinking of God and chanting his divine name, when the tenth month is completed, the child is expelled from the womb through the birth canal and takes birth outside.'"

"No matter how much love the parents may shower, the sorrows in childhood will be unbearable. It is guaranteed that various kinds of sorrow will befall him both in his youth and old age. The body is nothing but a bundle of sorrow. Creatures experience joy and sorrow just because of the sense of 'I' in their bodies. The sorrow of birth and death is only limited to the body. The Atma (soul) is separate from the gross and subtle bodies and is eternal. We should understand this truth, give up our love of the physical body and live life as a knower of the Self.'

When we donate this body, which is only an illusion, after our death. It becomes useful to us, to the recipient, and to the world as a whole.

www.ingramcontent.com/pod-product-compliance
Lightning Source LLC
LaVergne TN
LVHW012340100826
845148LV00018B/2858

9781680379013